D1155236

Leadership through Mentoring

Leadership through Mentoring

The Key to Improving the Confidence and Skill of Principals

Phyllis A. Gimbel and Peter Gow

with

Samson Goldstein

ROWMAN & LITTLEFIELD
Lanham • Boulder • New York • London

Published by Rowman & Littlefield
An imprint of The Rowman & Littlefield Publishing Group, Inc.
4501 Forbes Boulevard, Suite 200, Lanham, Maryland 20706
www.rowman.com

6 Tinworth Street, London SE11 5AL, United Kingdom

Copyright © 2021 by Phyllis A. Gimbel and Peter Gow.

All rights reserved. No part of this book may be reproduced in any form or by any
electronic or mechanical means, including information storage and retrieval systems,
without written permission from the publisher, except by a reviewer who may quote
passages in a review.

British Library Cataloguing in Publication Information Available

Library of Congress Cataloging-in-Publication Data

Names: Gimbel, Phyllis A., author. | Gow, Peter, author.
Title: Leadership through mentoring : the key to improving the confidence and skill of
    principals / Phyllis A. Gimbel and Peter Gow with Samson Goldstein.
Description: Lanham, Maryland : Rowman & Littlefield, 2021. | Includes bibliographical
    references and index. | Summary: "Leadership through Mentoring shows how
    effectiveness, vision, and engagement can be grown through intentional, supportive
    guidance and wise counsel, leading to longer and more successful principal tenures
    and significant improvements in school performance" — Provided by publisher.
Identifiers: LCCN 2021014647 (print) | LCCN 2021014648 (ebook) |
    ISBN 9781475853438 (cloth) | ISBN 9781475853445 (paperback) |
    ISBN 9781475853452 (ebook)
Subjects: LCSH: School principals—In-service training—United States. | Mentoring in
    education—United States. | School management and Organization—United States.
Classification: LCC LB1738.5 .G49 2021 (print) | LCC LB1738.5 (ebook) |
    DDC 371.2/011—dc23
LC record available at https://lccn.loc.gov/2021014647
LC ebook record available at https://lccn.loc.gov/2021014648

♾️™ The paper used in this publication meets the minimum requirements of American
National Standard for Information Sciences—Permanence of Paper for Printed Library
Materials, ANSI/NISO Z39.48-1992.

Contents

Acknowledgments

We would like to thank Michael J. Connnelly, PhD, Assistant Director, Massachusetts School Administrators Association (MSAA) and his team of mentors at MSAA. Dr. Connelly's expertise in mentoring new school leaders was instrumental in the foundation of this book.

We also wish to express our gratitude to Tom Koerner, PhD, Vice President/Senior Executive Editor/Education Division, Rowman & Littlefield Publisher, for his patience, guidance, and responsiveness. We also appreciate the efforts and guidance of Carlie Wall, Managing Editor, Rowman & Littlefield Publisher. Samson Goldstein, our graduate research assistant from Bridgewater State University, provided us with peace of mind with his timely work on the manuscript. We appreciate his diligence.

We thank the trustees and administrations of Bridgewater State University and One Schoolhouse for providing us with the time and support to bring this project to fruition. We believe that this book represents and furthers the missions of both institutions to support education and educators and to make all schools better for all children.

Introduction

Why Mentoring?

"I know it's only 10 minutes before home room, but the bus driver wants you."

"Also, a parent called about safety because she heard on the news about a bullying incident between two middle school girls that resulted in a fist fight. She wants to meet with you to find out what you are doing about bullying."

"And the science teacher is out today. He just called to say he thought he could make it to school, but he feels too sick—and we don't have a substitute."

The administrative assistant conveyed all of this to the new principal about forty-five minutes prior to the beginning of the school day at the middle school. So how is the new principal going to deal with these events before the school day begins? To whom can the principal turn regarding what to tackle first and how? This principal needs a mentor.

Today's new principals need to hit the halls running, ready to lead their staffs to accelerate the improvement of teaching and learning. Many are left to learn on the job (Southern Regional Education Board [SREB], 2016). It doesn't take long for new principals to feel overwhelmed by things coming at them from all directions—especially in the first two years, as they are trying to develop their own leadership skills.

One new principal said that he was happy to have a mentor, someone who would not judge him. Having been thirty years old when he was hired, he had been concerned that all constituencies—families, teachers, students—might question "whether or not he was right for the job." He said that his mentor, acting as a sounding board and a support, helped remove that insecurity—which he called "invaluable" (P. Gimbel, personal communication, January 7, 2020) in helping alleviate much of his insecurity.

In his 2015 report, *Developing Excellent School Principals to Advance Teaching and Learning; Considerations for State Policy*, Paul Manna suggests that today's school principal serves in an exceedingly and increasingly demanding role. Technology advancement and supporting diverse student populations, Manna claims, are challenges for many new principals.

In addition to school management, principals today are accountable for the ten professional standards for educational leaders adopted in 2015 by the National Policy Board for Educational Administration. These standards (see table 0.1) require new principals to lead their staffs in the improvement of teaching and learning. Additionally, the National Conference of State Legislatures suggests using statewide leadership standards to guide administrator evaluations (Shelton, 2013).

Often, when newly licensed principals begin their first job, they are left alone, without any kind of professional support from colleagues in similar roles. When asked what they need to sustain themselves, principals overwhelmingly report that they would benefit from ongoing support from peers through relevant discussion and collaboration (School Leaders Network, 2014).

NEED FOR MENTORING

It is widely believed, and research supports the idea, that a good principal is the key to a successful school (Branch et al., 2013) and that stability from retaining the same leader over time contributes to a school's success. Principals are second only to teachers when it comes to impact on student achievement in school (Aldrich, 2018; Leithwood et al., 2004; Superville, 2019).

But nearly half of new principals leave their schools after three years. In 2013, the National Center for Educational Statistics revealed that 70 percent of principals have spent less than five years at their current schools and that 20 percent of principals step down each year. Principal turnover has both academic and financial costs. Districts can spend as much as $75,000 to prepare, hire, and place a principal into a position (Superville, 2019). So why do districts and states not see the wisdom of spending a few thousand dollars on mentorship to increase the chances of a successful, longer-term principalship?

Table 0.1 Professional Standards for Educational Leaders (2015)

STANDARD	Area of Leadership	Description
1	Mission, Vision, and Core Values	Effective educational leaders develop, advocate, and enact a shared mission, vision, and core values of high-quality education and academic success and well-being of each student.
2	Ethics and Professional Norms	Effective educational leaders act ethically and according to professional norms to promote each student's academic success and well-being.
3	Equity and Cultural Responsiveness	Effective educational leaders strive for equity of educational opportunity and culturally responsive practices to promote each student's academic success and well-being.
4	Curriculum, Instruction, and Assessment	Effective educational leaders develop and support intellectually rigorous and coherent systems of curriculum, instruction, and assessment to promote each student's academic success and well-being.
5	Community of Care and Support for Students	Effective educational leaders cultivate an inclusive, caring, and supportive school community that promotes the academic success and well-being of each student.
6	Professional Capacity of School Personnel	Effective educational leaders develop the professional capacity and practice of school personnel to promote each student's academic success and well-being.
7	Professional Community for Teachers and Staff	Effective educational leaders foster a professional community of teachers and other professional staff to promote each student's academic success and well-being.
8	Meaningful Engagement of Families and Community	Effective educational leaders engage families and the community in meaningful, reciprocal, and mutually beneficial ways to promote each student's academic success and well-being.
9	Operations and Management	Effective educational leaders manage school operations and resources to promote each student's academic success and well-being.
10	School Improvement	Effective educational leaders act as agents of continuous improvement to promote each student's academic success and well-being.

Source: "Professional Standards for Educational Leaders," National Policy Board for Educational Administration (2015).

In "Lessons in Leadership: 4 Perspectives Taking Top Administrators to The Next Level," Riddell (2019) points out that 35 percent of principals remain in their position for two years or less. Learning Policy Institute (LPI) research, according to Riddell, suggests that the job of principal is overwhelming without adequate support.

The first two years of a principal's tenure are critical. Studies indicate that this period determines whether principals develop confidence and competence as school leaders or leave their positions (Leithwood, 2005). Making sense of one's first year as a school leader is challenging, and school principals would benefit from clear and consistent feedback on their handling of daily demands; without professional mentorship a new principal may not have access to this type of assistance (Gimbel & Kefor, 2018).

To prepare aspiring school leaders for such challenges, university schools of education and state licensing boards require aspiring principals to complete rigorous state-approved, competency-based, internship-culminating licensure programs prior to their first position (Gimbel & Kefor, 2018). Despite such academic preparation, when the National Association of Elementary School Principals polled a panel of new principals, 40 percent felt only "fairly prepared" or "not prepared" for their first day on the job (Superville, 2015). The required formal learning ends at the schoolhouse door, just when a new principal most needs responsive, in-the-moment support.

In a *SmartBrief* survey conducted by the Association for Supervision and Curriculum Development in 2015, 95.85 percent of educators surveyed agreed that principals need supplemental, on-the-job training. A formal mentoring program that pairs an experienced school leader and a novice principal can be invaluable to those who are beginning their school leadership positions.

Reducing teacher turnover is a compelling reason to keep school principals in their positions. Researchers now estimate that 44 percent of teachers will leave within the first five years of teaching (Whitaker et al., 2019). Teachers exiting the profession cite a lack of administrative support as one of the top reasons for attrition (Abitabile, 2020). When teachers are more satisfied with their jobs, Abitabile claims, they are more likely to stick with teaching, and it is a crucial part of the principal's job to seek out ways to increase teacher satisfaction by building supportive relationships and strong professional cultures.

Changes in leadership affect student achievement, teacher turnover, and school culture. In 2015, the Association for Supervision and Curriculum Development (ASCD) *SmartBrief* surveyed principals regarding job longevity. Just over a quarter of the respondents claimed that "being provided professional networks to engage with like practitioners" would encourage them to stay in their jobs as principal. Almost 23 percent of the responding principals said that being "provided ongoing, transformative professional development" would contribute to their willingness to remain in their current position (Association for Supervision and Curriculum Development [ASCD], 2015).

Principals who have had mentors are less stressed and stay longer, even if they are in low-income communities, where educator turnover is highest (Toner, 2019). In 2019, the National Association of Secondary School Principals (NASSP) and the LPI partnered to conduct a year-long study of principal turnover. The literature review conducted by LPI revealed that among the main reasons that principals leave their job are inadequate preparation and professional development.

Additionally, in focus group feedback from the administrators who participated in the second phase of the research, participants said the support they need includes high-quality professional learning opportunities with strong mentors and/or internships (Levin et al., 2019). Furthermore, many of these principal participants expressed gratitude for the mentors and colleagues who had guided and supported them through new experiences and difficult times. One participant said, "You have to have a trusted mentor or someone else that's across town that you can call, that can just understand the shoes you're walking in" (p. 11).

Johanek & Spero (*ASCD SmartBrief*, November 13, 2019) claim that a silent crisis of principal turnover is undermining school improvement efforts and that leadership is a key ingredient to success. They point to a 2013 Wallace Foundation study that found that more effective principals correlate to lower teacher turnover and increased teacher satisfaction.

A number of states have developed legislation ratifying formal mentoring and induction programs to support and retain new school principals. Education departments in some of these states try to collaborate with their local school administrators' associations to train retired school principals to become mentors. Examples of such efforts will be discussed in chapters 4 and 8.

Based on our research and on our own professional experience as school leaders, we believe that the development and implementation of a strong and effective principal mentorship program must be a district, state, and even national priority. As schools are weakened by teacher and principal turnover, we must find ways to build the capacity and confidence of building-level leaders to respond to the increasingly complex challenges that face them in their daily work to build stable, responsive, cultures of teaching, learning, and living in their schools.

In the following chapters we discuss:

Definition of Mentoring
Trust, Communication and Relationship Building
The Job Is Overwhelming
The Mentor Pathway
The Vermont Principals' Association Initiative
The Massachusetts School Administrators Association Initiative
Lessons from the 2020 Massachusetts Mentor Survey
Making Sense of Mentor Voices from Vermont and Massachusetts
Common Challenges for First-Year Principals
First-Year Challenges and the Mentoring Process
The Importance of Trust in Principals
About the NASSP and the LPI Research

Chapter 1

Definition of Mentoring

What precisely is mentoring? "Mentoring" is a term that defines a relationship between a less experienced mentee or protégé and a more experienced mentor. The mentoring relationship is between two people, typically face to face, for a long-term period and endeavors to expand a mentee's professional, academic, or personal development (Gimbel & Kefor, 2018). The role of mentor is supportive and not evaluative. Mentors train and instruct new school leaders through listening, questioning, and nonevaluative feedback, offering professional guidance as well as crucial emotional support based on their own experiences (New Hampshire Association of School Principals [NHASP], 2014a).

A principal mentor, usually a recently retired principal who has been trained in the process, has knowledge and experience in an area and shares it with the person being mentored, a novice school principal in a new position. A high-quality principal mentoring program is tailored to both individual needs and the cultural and/or strategic needs of the district. Throughout this book we use the terms "new principal" and "mentee" interchangeably to refer to the new school leader.

PURPOSES OF THE MENTOR PROGRAM

Mentor programs are often initiated with a primary goal of keeping principals in their schools in order to impact student achievement by strengthening cultures of learning. Feedback is necessary for school leaders to understand how effectively they are meeting the many daily demands they face. Engagement in collaborative professional exchanges helps build leadership confidence. The purposes of a mentor program are:

• To improve leadership performance
• To increase retention of new principals
• To promote the personal and professional well-being of beginning principals
• To satisfy mandated requirements for induction
• To transmit the culture of the school or district to beginning principals

WHAT ARE THE BENEFITS OF MENTORING?

A novice principal can feel isolated in an initial leadership position. Having access to someone who can keep confidentiality, who has an intimate knowledge of principalship, and who is a good listener can boost the novice's confidence. A trained mentor helps the new principal sort out what is important in the first few years of the principalship. Working with a mentor can offer a different perspective, an opportunity to reflect, an opportunity to help with communication with the greater school community, and an opportunity to offer praise when appropriate.

A mentor–mentee relationship can help the new principal (mentee) build self-confidence. Mentoring can promote self-analysis and reflection. Mentoring is a key psychosocial support (Smith & Piele, 2006): having an experienced, trusted confidante helps the new principal sort out personal stresses that come with the job. A veteran principal mentor can comment on practice, giving the new principal the "gift" of an outside, objective perspective.

The benefits of mentoring extend beyond those mentioned above. Some of the most important advantages of mentoring for novice principals include being able to ask questions and seek advice from someone who has already been a principal. The mentor may offer a different perspective by looking at a problem or issue with the benefit of being removed from the situation. Having dealt with similar or analogous situations and people, the mentor can help the mentee understand another point of view.

Since mentors are not like consultants, who work in a fee-for-specific-service model, they can assist in the overall development of mentees' leadership skills. Trained mentors can help the mentee communicate with teachers, staff, parents, students, and the community at large.

WHAT MAKES A GOOD MENTOR?

A mentor is assigned to assist the novice principal with the transition to be a new school leader. The mentor helps the new principal build connections with teachers, families, and students as well as passing on knowledge and experience. In chapters 5 and 6 we examine mentor training provided through several state administrators' associations.

A good mentor is someone who has done things you are doing and knows how to navigate through challenges and when and how to celebrate successes. A good mentor is someone who can candidly tell you how you are perceived by others. A good mentor is someone whom you can ask, without fear of judgment, how to overcome some of your worries and anxieties so that you can grow in your leadership position. A good mentor shows interest in the new principal's personal and professional life. A good mentor helps the novice principal build relationships with teachers.

"I think that my mentoring helps my mentee by her knowing I am there," one mentor said. We offer support (see next page).

An effective mentor

- Creates instructive challenges by helping the new principal understand and frame issues. A good mentor can help the new principal maintain focus on student learning as well as help with deep thinking on issues. Often, a new principal feels a problem needs to be solved or resolved quickly, but a mentor can ease this sense of urgency and angst.
- Facilitates, through dialogue, the development of a new principal's professional vision by asking questions about school demographics, parents, community, student achievement, goals, and resources, and helps in the formulation of ideas about how to approach the future.
- Offers new principals confidence in their own leadership, as exemplified by one mentor's statement: "I am not here to solve a problem for my mentees; my job is to empower my mentees to think *they* can solve the problem."
- Respects what the new principal is trying to do and helps push him or her to meet challenges and solve problems by offering different perspectives, as

shown by the questions this mentor posed: "What does the principal need to be doing? What is the principal's leadership? What is going to contribute to achieving those goals and what is not?"

- Listens but knows when to hold up a hand to make the new principal pause and listen back. One mentor's comments explained, "It gives the mentee freedom to walk through some possible solutions that he or she is thinking of in a safe place. There aren't any consequences to a thought experiment, and I think that is a real opportunity for mentees to try out 'this is what I am thinking of doing; this is the letter I want to write' and then to talk about those ripple effects before those effects actually occur."
- Collaborates, shares the air, and tries for reciprocal learning. As one mentor explained: "We are not there to give advice and to reminisce and tell stories about our experience. We are there to become very good cognitive coaches and to be questioners—to ask really good questions, to help our mentees think."
- Identifies and celebrates successes. A mentor commented, "When I ask her about walkthroughs, she tells me how great some of the classes are that she observes. I asked her if she acknowledges that to the teacher so that the teacher feels recognized."
- Frames instructive challenges. Another mentor explained: "I help her by pretty much using the Socratic Method—asking lots of questions."
- Gives a safe space to vent, air, complain, and feel shame. A mentor explained that his mentee's specific knowledge of education law policies, procedures, and the like is not as extensive as his and that "only through experience am I able to help her with the resources of time, availability, communication, and knowledge. She understands that she does not know as much about school law."
- Models best practices while still appreciating differences in leadership style. "You just want to help your mentees understand who they are and how that impacts how they make decisions, how that impacts how they lead with other people; but you can't really help them change who they are—and you don't want to."

HOW DOES A MENTOR OFFER SUPPORT?

"Offering support" is a broad term. Support to a new principal especially means being a confidante. A good mentor can offer support by:

- Attending fully, which means listening respectfully when a mentee needs to share concerns
- Responding empathetically in such a way that the new principal's feelings, frustrations, and experiences are acknowledged
- Reviewing and coordinating schedules to identify times that may be devoted to addressing pressing personal or professional concerns
- Suggesting and offering helpful resources
- Providing helpful information

HOW DOES A MENTOR CREATE CHALLENGE?

According to Wellman & Lipton (2003), effective mentors help the new principal set high but attainable expectations, assist with meeting goals, encourage collaborative opportunities, and model a professional identity.

Meeting the National Policy Board for Educational Administration's Ten Professional Standards for Educational Leaders is a challenge for any new principal. How might a new principal decide which of the Standards to tackle first? And how many in one year? The good mentor can help the novice principal set realistic goals.

Since the Conference of State Legislatures suggested using statewide leadership standards to guide administrative evaluations (Shelton, 2013), mentors can help mentees decide which of those standards to focus on. State standards usually center around instructional leadership, management and operations, family and community engagement, and professional culture.

A GOOD MENTOR HELPS RETAIN TEACHERS

With principals being pulled in many different directions and answering to so many stakeholders and constituencies, nurturing teachers may not always have a principal's attention as a top priority, and a mentor can emphasize the importance of this role. Research also suggests that principal behaviors have a significant impact when teachers are deciding whether to leave their schools (Abitabile, 2020).

Mentors are experienced principals themselves and, as such, can advise new principals on how to keep teachers in their schools. Abitabile claims that newer teachers want to interact with their principals considerably more than do their veteran counterparts (p. 52). Research and experience suggest that a new principal must make sure to be visible to teachers. By being seen, principals can engage teachers in conversation and promote a collegial relationship, fostering a positive culture.

A good mentor will also advise a new principal to foster connections between teachers, especially with those teachers who are positive about the school and the students. A good mentor will explain to the new principal the value of recognizing when teachers do something great in or outside the classroom. A good mentor will help the new principal offer timely, honest feedback to teachers. All these strategies help build a positive principal–teacher relationship.

Chapter 2

Trust, Communication, and Relationship Building

TRUST AS A RELATIONSHIP BUILDER

As one middle school teacher said, "Trust is built by learning to depend on the principal: as school leader; as a 'broker' to respond to needs of the teachers for resources and classroom management tips; and overall being there for teachers, which allows them to do their job" (Gimbel, 2003, p. xiii).

Trust is "a leveraging tool and the foundation on which the principal can build and sustain one-to-one relationships with his or her teaching staff, especially when the principal is new to the school" (Gimbel, 2003, p. 54). The same applies to a newly established mentor-mentee relationship. When there is trust in a school setting or in a mentor relationship, teachers and mentee principals are more willing to be honest and open with one another. In a February 22, 2018, ASCD *SmartBrief* poll, respondents claimed that advice on building relationships is the most important thing they can offer new principals in their quest to build principal-teacher trust.

"Trust grows as members of a community have positive experiences" (Berg et al., 2018, p. 58). "Sustaining a trusting environment within a school is an ongoing challenge, for there are ebbs and flows in communication" (Gimbel & Leana, 2013, p. 144). This can also occur in the mentor-mentee relationship.

So how can mentors build trust with their mentees? Is the mentor pushing the mentee to solve or resolve the problem by considering a different perspective? Is the mentor showing respect for what the mentee is trying to do? Does the mentor acknowledge feelings, frustrations, and experiences? Does the mentor celebrate successes?

Does the mentor show interest in the mentee's personal and professional life? Is the mentor allowing the mentee to have a safe space to vent, air, complain, and feel shame, thus reassuring the mentee of confidentiality? How is the mentor offering feedback? Does the mentor listen but know when to encourage the mentee to pause and listen? All these communication questions focus on engendering trust between the mentor and mentee.

In turn, carefully cultivated trust between mentors and mentees can strengthen principals' own trust-building behaviors as they work to create relationships in their school communities, especially with teachers. By incorporating the lessons in trust learned in the mentoring process, principals can reduce the chances for missteps as they work on challenging situations.

BUILDING TRUST WHILE MAKING DIFFICULT DECISIONS

A new principal often enters the position having been handed a pre-set agenda regarding areas that have been identified as problems by a predecessor or even the superintendent. Sometimes this agenda includes a mandate for drastic action that could, however well intended, have dire consequences for individuals and might put the new principal in a difficult position vis-à-vis school constituencies. Here is where mentoring can pay off especially handsomely.

In many cases the agenda handed to the new principal involves dealing with teachers regarded as not "up to snuff," even when the teacher evaluation process has not resulted in specific recommendations for action. The new principal must assess the situation and decide what must be done, at the risk of coming off as the "bad guy" or "hired gun" to other teachers looking on. A single decision, hastily made, can completely deplete most of any political or personal capital that the new principal might have with the faculty.

For example, when one new high school principal was hired, the superintendent told the new principal that a world language teacher was underperforming, and the previous principal did not fire him. The superintendent wanted the new principal, within the first year of her principalship, to get rid of the teacher.

Fortunately, the new principal had a mentor, so she asked her mentor how to weed out the underperforming teacher. The mentor realized that his mentee was about to confront conflict early in her principalship. He also knew that their own relationship was new, and he wanted to build trust with his mentee. So, what could he do?

He was candid with her, asking her how she would feel if teachers who liked the underperforming teacher were to turn against her. He also asked her how she would handle conflict. The mentor explained that his mentee might feel some fear in this situation, but that when some of the teachers and staff see her confront this situation, of which they may also be aware, it might build trust—as perhaps they, like the superintendent, have been awaiting someone who could and would act decisively.

The mentor also suggested his mentee read about the teacher's evaluations, familiarize herself with the district's teacher evaluation policy, visit the teacher's classroom informally as a walkthrough, and then confer with the teacher about the evaluation process before a formal evaluation. The mentor did not tell her how to fire the teacher. Instead, the mentor provided resources.

The new principal followed the mentor's suggestions. Her visits to the teacher's classroom helped her gain a perspective that she claims she would not have considered had she not had a mentor. Although the new principal suggested strategies for the teacher to improve, she soon realized that this underperforming world language teacher was not well suited to teach high school students but seemed as though he would be effective with middle school students.

After several classroom visits and the formal teacher evaluation process, the mentee suggested that the teacher apply for a middle school position that was opening in a neighboring town. He did, and he was offered and accepted that position. The mentee celebrated her own ability to take time and think deeply on this problem of practice. The mentee also gained trust from her teachers as they applauded her ability to help the teacher find another, more appropriate position.

COMMUNICATING WELL IN THE
MENTOR–MENTEE SPACE

What is effective communication? *Merriam Webster*'s definition is to "transmit information, thought, or feeling so that is it is satisfactorily received or understood" (Gimbel et al., 2016, p. 17). This applies to the mentor-mentee relationship.

The mentor needs to communicate effectively with the mentee to build a trusting, confidential relationship. Mentees may work carefully with mentors to craft what they want to say, but they have "little idea of how accurately the message is received or understood by others" (p. 17). Mentors need to help mentees understand how what they say may be interpreted by various audiences. In order to build a collaborative faculty-staff relationship with the goal of building a shared vision, effective communication is critical.

Communication is a building block in the mentor–mentee relationship. Trust rests on how the mentor is perceived by the mentee. Many problems, challenges, and decision points that the mentee encounters center around effective communication. The mentor–mentee relationship is linked to the mentor's ability to communicate with the mentee—and the mentee's success as a new principal rests on communication. As Art Petty (January 29, 2020) wrote in the ASCD *SmartBrief*:

> It turns out, everything important in our careers and working lives takes place in one or more challenging conversations, and every communication encounter is critical if you lead. And while we continuously strive via books, articles, and courses to identify and replicate the secret ingredients of great leadership, too often, we ignore the centrality of communication effectiveness to effective leadership.

Therefore, it is incumbent upon the mentor to model and promote effective communication. What are the strategies for doing this?

The critical skill in effective communication is listening. That means clearing the mentor's own mind to focus on the mentee. This shows respect and empathy, both critical leadership skills. If the mentor models these skills, the mentee can learn to do likewise. The mentor needs to work hard to understand the mentee's situation and to see a situation or issue through the mentee's eyes. This makes the mentee feel acknowledged and "felt," engendering trust and enhancing the mentor–mentee relationship.

LISTENING: AN ESSENTIAL COMMUNICATION TOOL

Listening is an important component of the mentoring relationship. Wellman & Lipton (2003) devised a verbal tool kit for active listening whose components are:

- Pause
- Paraphrase

- Inquire
- Probe
- Extend

According to Wellman & Lipton (2003), pausing is used after asking a question or after receiving a response. This pause enables the mentor to frame his or her own language. The pause often occurs between the paraphrase and the next question. Paraphrasing signals listening, acknowledges clarity, and summarizes and organizes thoughts. It shifts the level of abstraction.

Inquiring means asking without implied judgment. If you have a preferred response, it is not inquiry. Probing is asking who, what, where, when, and how. Extending is giving information, framing expectations, and providing resources (Wellman & Lipton, 2003). All of these are active listening techniques the mentor can use to engage the mentee.

A few years after Wellman and Lipton devised their verbal tool kit, the Center for Adaptive Schools (2006) asserted what they called the "norms of collaboration." These norms offer mentors ways to listen to their mentee so that the mentee feels the relationship is collaborative; and therefore, the mentee is willing to share thoughts with the mentor. As a bonus, these norms can also be valuable for the mentee to use in the school to build a collaborative community.

These are the norms of collaboration:

- Promote a spirit of inquiry by showing interest
- Pause to see if the listener wants to say anything or to be sure the listener hears you
- Paraphrase to verify understanding
- Probe by composing probing questions
- Pay attention to self and others
- Presume positive interactions by not assuming the mentee thinks negatively
- Put ideas on the table by offering multiple perspectives

LISTENING PLUS GREAT FEEDBACK = TRUST

The mentee in the "teacher-firing" scenario tackled a tough situation in the first year of her tenure. With the mentor's support, the mentee was willing to tackle a problem that the predecessor had ignored. The mentee offered candid feedback on the teacher's performance by communicating clearly and helping that teacher become self-aware. The mentee in turn identified the teacher's strengths, explaining that the teacher seemed well suited to teaching middle school students. The outcome inspired confidence and hope that things in the high school would change for the better (Jones & Vari, 2019).

The same applies in a mentor–mentee relationship. Providing feedback is a delicate form of communication, and relationships can crumble if the feedback is not supportive and objective.

Bell (2020) has some ideas about offering feedback from principal to teacher. These ideas are also applicable to the mentor–mentee relationship. The first feedback strategy Bell suggests is validation, by looking for ways to encourage the good work happening in the school. Focusing on what is strong instead of what is wrong will allow the mentee to see the results of initiatives that the mentee has been working hard to implement in the school. Bell says that people need to know where they are excelling, and having the mentor recognize the contribution the mentee made to the school is a culture builder.

According to Bell, the most common reason to offer feedback is to suggest refinement of some action or pattern of response. But Bell claims that this type of feedback is "usually delivered in a way that misses the opportunity for growth." Bell suggests being sure that the mentor validates what the mentee is doing well prior to mentioning any small adjustments that could be made. Finally, Bell says that when a behavior needs to be corrected, feedback should be direct, clearly describing the behavior with suggestions on another type of action (Bell, 2020).

Daskal (2020) also offers further suggestions related to feedback; more specifically to helping a struggling employee. The first thing Daskal says to do is to identify the issue so the mentor can understand the root cause of the problem. When that can be done, the mentor and mentee can work together to develop solutions that may work in the future.

The next step Daskal suggests is to communicate clearly by offering candid feedback to increase self-awareness. Then, Daskal explains, focus on the facts in order to prevent the mentee from taking the feedback personally. Give clear examples of the behavior or the issue at hand to demonstrate how these examples affect the mentee's status as new principal. Then, work on a solution together by giving the mentee ownership of the situation, allowing for extra motivation for improvement.

Keep the expectations clear, Daskal recommends, so that the mentee knows what is expected in the future. Since "behavior responds to encouragement and rewards" (Daskal, 2020), offer praise and recognition for the efforts the mentee is putting forth. Finally, once the mentor and mentee have formulated a plan, create a follow-up schedule to check on how things are going.

Mentors themselves suggest the following tips for offering feedback to mentees:

- Be positive
- Be immediate
- Be honest
- Be specific
- Offer suggestions, not answers
- Be empathetic
- Be growth-oriented; the primary purpose of feedback is not assessment but improvement
- Be reasonable
- Be objective
- Offer a useful strategy or tool (Hoff, 2019)

The National Association of Elementary School Principals (NAESP) (2008) suggests specific questions that mentors can pose to their mentees. By listening carefully to a mentee's response, the mentor can develop ideas for feedback to the mentee that can be applied to specific situations.

QUESTIONS RELATED TO GOALS

- What do you want to accomplish, both short and long term?
- Is the goal realistic? What are the major constraints in meeting the goal?

QUESTIONS ON OPTIONS FOR ACTIONS

- What options do you have?
- What if?
- Would you like another suggestion?

QUESTIONS ON THE MENTEE'S WILL TO SUCCEED

- What are you going to do and when will you do it?
- Will this meet your goal?
- What obstacles do you expect to face, and how will you overcome them?

TAKEAWAYS: FEEDBACK GUIDELINES

Mentors need to be trained in how to listen and how to offer objective, supportive feedback. Here are some guidelines for mentors to give feedback:

- Build rapport with your mentee
- Be kind and totally honest at the same time
- Focus on behaviors and not personality
- Consider the timing of the feedback
- Make constructive comments
- Ask for feedback on your feedback

Chapter 3

The Job Is Overwhelming

"Well, I don't know what to do. Parents are so angry with me for not doing anything about the middle school students who are planning to bring water balloons to school. I didn't even find out about this until the custodian mentioned that he heard two students talking about it. I only wish I had someone to talk with about this issue," the new middle school principal muttered quietly.

At another school, the teachers' union representative told the new high school principal, "You can't make us stay fifteen minutes longer at the faculty meeting just because you want us to discuss the new schedule now that we worked with all stakeholders to start school later in the morning." The new principal did not know how to respond to the representative, who was also a music teacher in the school. "If only I could have run this by someone I trust and from whom I could seek advice," the high school principal thought. "What did I get myself into when I signed the contract to become the new principal?"

The job of principal today is overwhelming. Principals today are charged with implementing the ten National Policy Board for Educational Administration (NPBEA) professional standards for education leaders (2015). Standard areas include:

1. Mission, vision, and core values
2. Ethics and professional norms
3. Equity and cultural responsiveness

4. Curriculum, instruction, and assessment
5. Community of care and support for students
6. Professional capacity of school personnel
7. Professional community for teachers and staff
8. Meaningful engagement of families and community
9. Operations and management
10. School improvement

The demands on the principal increase when adding school safety, mental health, and the challenges of meeting the needs of a diverse student body.

Superville (2019) tells the story of a principal who left the position after five years. She said that the stresses built up "over a two-year period, including changes to how schools are graded and held accountable, his mother's death, a bus accident that injured students and staff, a lack of support to address student mental health needs, and long hours" (p. 10). The work took a toll on the principal's well-being.

Did this principal have a mentor who tried to sort out what was important to do and what could wait? Did he have someone to listen to his personal and professional struggles? And, if he did, how much time could he devote to face-to-face meetings with his mentor, given the many competing and often legitimately urgent demands on his time?

HELP, PLEASE

"Please slow down and take a deep breath," a mentor advised a mentee. "But I have five goals for this year, how can I slow down?" the mentee retorted. "Well, what does your boss, the superintendent, want you to accomplish this year?" the mentor inquired. "I am not sure," the mentee replied.

In this instance, perhaps the superintendent has one goal and the mentee has four—or vice versa. Together, the mentor and mentee can work on how to assess the school culture and try to develop goals for the year. But when in their new relationship can the mentor and mentee discuss goal setting? Early summer meetings can allow for conversation about why the principal was hired and what the superintendent wants accomplished early in the principal's tenure. There is more about this in the next chapter.

THANK YOU FOR THE HELP

Another new principal wanted to require all teachers to submit weekly lesson plans to the assistant principals. This had been a top item on a list of things to accomplish in the first year. Fortunately, this principal had a trained mentor who reminded the mentee that to build a collaborative culture, it would be necessary to include teachers in decision-making whenever possible. The mentor said this would take longer, but that it would engender trust in her as a new principal.

About a month later, a few teachers informed the new principal that, although it was an extra step, they were happy she asked them if submitting lesson plans weekly would enhance teaching and learning. The teachers said that by asking for their opinions, they felt validated professionally.

The new principal learned about the value of soliciting input from teachers in order to build a collaborative culture. Had there not been someone with whom to consult on this issue, this principal might have begun her tenure by making a decision that could have come across as mistrustful of teachers and could have impeded any future effort to build trust. "The typical first-year principal wants to show everyone what s/he knows, but the most effective way to lead is to empower others. I learned that from my mentor" (Gill, 2019, p. 44).

Principals need high quality, intentional support that meets their needs (Rowland, 2017). With such support, in a mentoring program, principals can strengthen their performance and feel more confident in their leadership, making them feel more secure in their positions. This of course strengthens the cultures of their schools, yielding direct results for teachers and students as learning communities become more confident and effective. Yet, as Rowland points out, states and districts tend to overlook the need to support school leaders once the new principal is installed.

In February of 2019, The Wallace Foundation published *Sustaining a Principal Pipeline* (Anderson & Turnbull, 2019), which presents a compelling rationale for investment in New Leader Induction programs. The report is based on the Wallace Foundation study, which showed that school principal participants felt that no matter how strong their preparation was, they still needed support from a mentor as they "lived in" their new leadership positions.

CHALLENGES

Facing a new school and new challenges, novice principals need to be able to deflect the feeling of being overwhelmed and express their concerns to someone they can trust—someone in a mentoring position rather than someone who might be evaluating them. They need to be able to reflect and improve practice based on honest conversation and wise feedback without feeling the pressure of being evaluated.

Among the challenging issues a novice principal can face is bullying. According to Understood for All, Inc, in 2017, more than 70 percent of students said they have seen bullying in school. In one high school, a student spread rumors about another student via social media. The victim was ridiculed by peers, and the novice principal did not know how to handle the situation. Fortunately, the mentor asked the mentee questions about the two students involved. Through the conversation between mentor and mentee, the novice principal collaborated with teachers to draft behavioral expectations and how to meet them in school. Together, the novice principal and teachers encouraged students to speak up when they see or hear about bullying. If this novice principal had not had a mentor with whom to discuss the situation, the expectations might have taken longer to draft or may not even have been drafted at all.

As school began in another high school, a new principal considered an upcoming active shooter drill that had been planned with the local police department and scheduled prior to the new principal's arrival. The new principal was concerned about the drill perhaps being held too early in the school year. He spoke with his mentor, and together they decided it would be best to wait until later in the school year to have the drill.

The new principal felt it might be too traumatic for teenagers to hear the actual shots fired, and he wanted to acclimate himself to the school culture to prepare students and teachers for the drill. Along with his mentor, the new principal reviewed active shooter drills in other high schools and their impact on students. Without a mentor to help decide, the principal might have allowed the drill to go forward too soon in his tenure, creating angst for both teachers and students.

MAKING COMMUNICATION WORK
IN COMPLICATED LIVES

Another principal said she was pleased with her mentor, as he understood that she had three children under the age of seven while her husband commuted to another state three days a week, so she had very little time to meet face to face. Together, they decided to meet face to face every two months and that each week she would phone the mentor from her car while driving home.

One mentor said her mentee was too busy to meet about a problem that had occurred in his school. One of his teachers was accused of making inappropriate comments to a student. The mentor, who was out of town when this happened, used an internet communication app to connect with her mentee. The mentor said that the app enabled her to connect her mentee with other principals who had similar issues. She was also able to send her mentee links to pertinent articles. The mentor said she uses this app when her mentees need multiple perspectives or resources or time to sort things out.

Virtual modalities for establishing communication between the mentor and mentee such as smartphone or internet services like Zoom, Skype, and others are especially useful in rural locations or where the mentor and mentee are situated far apart.

MENTOR AND SUPERINTENDENT

What we have not yet discussed is how mentors are accountable to their superintendents. Time logs are a common method for informing superintendents about the progress of the mentor initiative in the district; these logs may be part of the district induction program. Mentor logs include names of the mentor and mentee, a description of the activity, date, and time spent.

The Denver Public Schools, for example, utilize a mentor log that requires at least twenty hours per semester of mentor–mentee interaction.

The log contains the following information:

- Mentor and mentee names, their school, the semester
- Activity or meeting name and description; what was accomplished?
- Date and hours; total hours

Such logs not only track interaction but can also help the superintendent understand more about the mentor–mentee relationship. The superintendent needs to know if the relationship is helping the new principal in his or her position in order to build the case for the mentoring budget.

Some mentor programs require the mentor to define an action plan based upon the needs of the mentee. In these instances, the mentor submits a plan for the mentor year that encompasses the mentor's vision, goals, plans, timeline, anticipated obstacles, outcomes, evidence to be sought, and ways to celebrate success (National Association of Elementary School Principals [NAESP], 2008).

The New Hampshire School Leaders Program (2014) uses a mentor evaluation form that mentees complete. The form asks mentees to rate their mentors on fulfilling their responsibilities on a scale of 1 to 5, with "5" meaning "very often." The categories of the evaluation ask how frequently the mentor assisted the mentee in these areas:

- Develop and follow an action plan
- Help you strengthen your leadership capacity
- Employ listening skills during your sessions
- Provide consultation and support to you
- Utilize data to assist in your growth
- Develop trust
- Cultivate your professional growth in accordance with professional standards
- Identify and build upon your strengths and leadership style
- Focus your vision on high quality instruction and improved student learning
- Maintain strict confidentiality
- Respond in a timely manner to your needs
- Encourage your reflection by posing thought-provoking questions
- Provide you with resources as needed
- Visit your work site when invited
- Help you build a professional network
- Make the necessary time commitment

The survey includes the following additional questions:

- What I appreciated most about my mentor was_____
- A suggestion I have for my mentor is_____
- Finally, I want to say_____
- May this evaluation be shared with your mentor?

IS MENTORING WIDESPREAD?

These scenarios and topics make a strong case for intentionally designed principal mentoring programs. The 2015 federal education law allows states to set aside funds for programs that are geared to principals, teacher-leaders, principal supervisors and leadership development (Superville, 2017). Some of these funds, however, may be eliminated, and some states are reluctant to initiate mentor programs for new principals. The reasons for such reluctance seem to be grounded in budgetary concerns rather than considered decisions based on educational goals or best practices.

There are some states, however, that have developed legislation ratifying formal mentoring and induction programs for new school principals, hoping to support and retain these school leaders. As of 2015–2016, only twenty states and districts required some form of professional support for new principals (Goldrick, 2016). In a few of these states, such as Massachusetts and Vermont, the state associations train retired principals to serve as mentors. These initiatives are described in chapters 5 and 6.

Chapter 4

The Mentor Pathway

THE BEGINNING OF THE MENTOR YEAR

How to begin? What to say? What is the entry plan? How will we relate to one another? These are some of the questions a trained mentor may contemplate. Although the mentor has been a principal and may even have had prior experience as a mentor, the early stages of the mentor–mentee relationship are fragile. Both the mentor and the mentee may be uneasy, as they do not know each other.

To build a relationship early in the mentor year, the mentor can listen carefully to the new principal, the mentee, to build confidence. By narrating some of the problems of practice the mentor has experienced in his or her previous leadership positions, the mentor helps the mentee become more at ease and more inclined to share apprehensions and concerns.

ENTRY PLANNING AND INITIAL MENTOR MEETINGS

Much of the first meeting of the mentor and mentee is devoted to entry planning. As Jentz (2009) writes, "As a first time principal or administrator, you'll be on the receiving end of the dynamics of authority in your interaction with others, those who report to you and others whose lives are touched by your decisions. When you're with people who work under you, you'll see, hear, and feel conversation change from inclusion to exclusion in words, tone, demeanor, and content" (p. 56).

This is what happened to a new principal upon entering the teachers' lounge in the school. When the new principal entered the room, conversation stopped. The teachers in the lounge just looked at one another. The new principal immediately felt isolated and disconnected from the teachers and decided to talk with the mentor about these feelings.

Explaining to the mentee that teachers often change the subject or stop talking and smile when an administrator enters a room, the mentor suggested making light of it and acknowledging the awkwardness of the situation in a humorous way, thereby letting teachers know that the new principal understood that "their" territory was being "invaded." This, then, is a dynamic of authority (Jentz, 2009).

As Heifetz and Linsky (2002) and Jentz (2009) point out, the new principal will encounter lots of problems that are confusing because they don't have easy answers. This could cause a feeling of powerlessness in taking on the significant matters that might have led the mentee to accept the position. This is just one of many reasons a mentor is invaluable at the beginning of the school year.

Sometimes people think the beginning of a leadership position has a honeymoon phase, but because a school community is made up of teachers, students, staff, parents, and the community at large, dealing with so many stakeholders while trying to establish oneself is daunting. A mentor who can help the new principal sort things out, prioritize issues, and take a step back will allow the mentee time to reflect. Having a supportive mentor can offer the mentee opportunity to consider using and then design an entry plan, a "blueprint" to guide the mentee in his or her first year as an administrator.

The optimal time for the first mentor meeting would be in the summer preceding the school year. At this time the mentor can ask probing questions to get the mentee thinking about his or her new role as school leader. These and all meetings will naturally be driven by the needs of the mentee. The mentor needs to reassure the mentee that everything said between them is confidential. In order to keep the conversation focused on the thoughts, feelings, and job challenges of the mentee, certain questions can be posed by the mentor.

The following questions have been adapted from National Association of Elementary School Principals (NAESP) (2008) suggestions and general sequence:

QUESTIONS TO GET THINGS STARTED

- What are you expecting to _____?
- How aware are you of _____?
- What might be the basis for the action you may take on _____?
- What might lead you to draw a conclusion or make the decision about _____?

QUESTIONS TO SUPPORT PLANNING

- As you think about the coming year, what are some surrounding dynamics that are influencing you?
- What are some of your perceptions about what is going on with _____?
- As we start to think about _____, what are some of the perspectives that will help us see a fuller view?
- What are some variables that might influence your actions and outcomes?
- How does the coming year connect with previous experiences?
- As you contemplate the coming year, where does it fit in the big picture of your life?
- What might we talk about that would be most useful to you?
- Describe some of the differences between what you planned and what might occur.
- What are some inferences you are making about____ and on what evidence do you base these?
- What are some variables that might affect the outcome?
- What are some new connections you will need to be making?
- What are some things you are taking away from this experience that will influence your future practice?

Carl Weingartner (2009) suggests some additional entry planning questions:

- What is the socioeconomic composition of the student population?
- What are the demographics of the community?
- Does the school community have safety issues?
- What does the history of student test data reflect?
- What is vested in the existing curriculum?

- How do you quickly identify the strengths and weaknesses in the curriculum?
- What are the demographics of the staff?
- Can you identify the leaders on your staff? The dissenters?
- Are those leaders supportive of your appointment?
- Can you identify teachers who are not performing up to expectations?
- Is the staff a cohesive team?
- What condition is the school in (buildings, grounds, maintenance)?
- Is the school attractive? Does it evoke a sense of pride?
- Do you know your community leaders? Are they supportive of your appointment to *their* school?
- Is the political structure of the community understood?

After a few months, the mentor relationship will be in the "middle stage" (NAESP, 2008). At this point, both the mentor and the mentee will begin to see patterns in the issues surrounding the new principal's leadership. So, it is time for the mentor to offer support, encouragement, and some nurturing. Not coincidentally, this is usually the time the mentee truly begins to see the mentor as a partner and colleague (NAESP, 2008).

At the final stage of the mentor pathway, the mentee has some understanding of the meaning of the relationship and knows how to ask for feedback from colleagues. The mentee has learned to think more deeply. And now, often, the mandated or funded year concludes, and the mentor departs before the "entire journey is over" (NAESP, 2008).

Several states are aware that that one year is not enough to help the new principal in his or her position. These states have mandated or recommended two years of mentoring. The states with required principal mentorship programs are shown in Table 4.1.

Table 4.1   State Principal Mentor Programs in the United States

Required, no minimum length (3)	Required for one year (11)	Required for two years (5)	Required for more than two years (1)
Colorado	Arkansas	California	Delaware
Pennsylvania	Iowa	Hawai'i	
Wisconsin	Kansas	Missouri	
	Maryland	New Jersey	
	Massachusetts	Vermont	
	New York		
	South Carolina		
	Texas		
	Utah		
	Virginia		
	West Virginia		

Note. "Illinois State law requires two years of support for new district superintendents and one year for school principals, but these mandates are contingent upon a level of state funding that has never materialized. Kentucky's principal internship program is currently suspended due to budget constraints. At least three additional states operate beginning school administrator induction programs, but do not require participation by educators or districts. For example, the Alabama New Principal Mentoring Program is an optional two-year coaching and support program supported by the state education department. LEAD Connecticut operates the Turnaround Principals Program aimed at low-achieving schools. New Mexico's School Leadership Institute provides 'a comprehensive and cohesive framework for preparing mentoring and providing professional development for principals.' Oregon awards competitive grants for new school administrator induction and mentoring, but does not require it statewide" (Goldrick, 2016, p. 10).
Source: NASSP Bulletin, 2018

IN SUM, PLANNING FOR MENTOR MEETINGS

- Mutual sharing
- Establishing a contact schedule
- Encouraging
- Sharing tips for building relationships with stakeholders
- Talking about professional goals

Chapter 5

The Vermont Principals'
Association Initiative

As mentioned in chapter 3, some states that require mentoring of new school principals call upon their state principal associations to train recently retired school principals as mentors. Massachusetts and Vermont are two such states. This chapter will discuss the Vermont Initiative, and the following chapter will explain the Massachusetts Initiative. Subsequent chapters will offer take-aways from both programs.

THE VERMONT INITIATIVE

In a study of new rural principals who had no access to an induction program, researchers found that after two years, a staggering 90 percent had moved to other positions or returned to teaching (Morford, 2002; NYC Leadership Brief, 2019). In 2011, Vermont educational leaders and the Vermont Principals' Association (VPA) recognized the increasing complexity of the principal's role and noticed that this transformation was affecting the retention of high-quality candidates (Gimbel & Kefor, 2018, p. 5).

Vermont lawmakers and educators partnered to design a bill to support new professional educators, principals, and technical center directors with mentors for the first two years in their new positions (p. 6). The bill, known in the state's educational community as Act 20, was put into effect in 2012 and calls for the following:

When a school district hires a principal or a technical center director who has not been employed previously in that capacity, the superintendent serving the district, in consultation with the Vermont Principals' Association, shall work to ensure that the new principal or technical center director receives mentoring supports during at least the first two years of employment. Mentoring supports shall be consistent with best practices, research-based approaches, or other successful models, and shall be identified jointly by the Vermont Principals' Association and the Vermont Superintendents Association. (VT LEG 269886.1. No. 20)

The basic qualifications for Vermont principal mentors, who are recently retired principals, include at least five years of experience as a school leader or director with such subskills as the abilities to listen, to help others reflect, and to demonstrate strong interpersonal skills, and to have had their own successful leadership experiences, to exhibit a professional demeanor, to have a strong knowledge of resources, and to possess strong problem-solving skills, and a proclivity for flexible thinking (NHASP, 2014b). The ability to maintain confidentiality is also imperative.

Vermont school superintendents have choices about how to pair mentors and novice principals as their mentees. They can match new principals with an in-district mentor, or they can reach out to the VPA. Sometimes there may not be an in-district person qualified to mentor. The VPA offers consultative services to superintendents and districts at no cost. Usually the VPA offers a choice among three qualified mentors to assist a new principal.

The mentors are compensated at the standard funding level of $3750 per program year (NHASP, 2014). Mentors in Vermont earn $65 per hour for personalized mentoring supports, which can include preparation for meetings, face-to-face meetings, and phone, email, or virtual meetings. Districts where new school leaders are employed must fund these costs, but there are multiple funding options available including grants, entitlement funds, and professional development monies (Gimbel & Kefor, 2018).

THE VPA TRAINING

Aspiring mentors, who can be retired school principals from both Vermont and New Hampshire, attend a three-day development training program. Topics addressed in the training are:

- The current educational landscape
- Mentor competencies

- Norms of collaboration
- Resources for mentors
- Gathering feedback and data through surveys
- Entry planning
- State Principal Evaluation Standards
- Articles supporting mentoring
- Reflective process through journaling (Gimbel & Kefor, 2018)

LET'S HEAR FROM SOME VERMONT MENTORS

Thus far we have talked about mentoring, but we have not heard directly from mentors. One of the authors of this book conducted a two-year, exploratory, phenomenological study exploring the perceptions of new principals and their assigned mentors in the VPA Initiative. The participants in the study discussed their mentor–mentee relationships and how these affect leadership practices (Gimbel & Kefor, 2018). A few of the mentor responses to some interview questions demonstrate a clearer understanding of how a trained mentor feels about his/her role.

Below are selected questions and responses from Vermont mentors:

1. *How do you help your mentee achieve his or her goals for the current year?*
2. *How does your mentoring help with your mentee's greatest challenge?*
3. *What is the most important thing your mentee is learning from you?*
4. *What could you not help your mentee with, and why not?*
5. *What suggestions would you have to enhance or improve the mentoring experience to reflect the Program goals?*
1. *How do you help your mentee achieve his or her goals for the current year?*

Mentor responses suggest that trust between the mentor and mentee needs to be built prior to helping the mentee work on achieving his or her specific goals. Building trust, according to these mentors, rests on building a relationship with the mentee by meeting regularly and by communicating as often as possible, even after school hours should the need arise.

One mentor responded in greater length as follows:

I do that as a first step by building a relationship that was founded in trust, and in the early part of the fall we walked around the school. I went to faculty meetings, and I tried to build up a context to understand what she was dealing with, and that was built over the first couple of months. One of the first things to do as a trained mentor is to examine the national standards for school principals, and my mentee prioritized what things she wanted to work on as well as setting a series of goals for herself, so I knew what it was she was trying to achieve.

The new prinicpal had come to this position after being a teacher and a curriculum leader in the district, and she had spent some time in central office as an assistant superintendent for curriculum and instruction, so she knew what was going on here, and her goals were established based upon two fundamental things that she saw.

The same mentor added:

One thing that she saw was the need for a cultural reset to re-create a sense of trust between and among the faculty and the principal in the building. Secondly, she wanted to set the framework for a school mission and a set of goals so she could build a foundation or framework for her second big goal of creating a school dedicated to innovation, reflection, and, you know, a collaborative design, those kinds of things, moving forward. And so much of our work throughout the year was based upon dealing with those two goals.

Another mentor said this about goal setting with their mentee:

I help her achieve her goals for the coming year by first meeting with her regularly; I think it is a communication thing—making sure the lines of communication are open all the time—which means after school hours, in the evenings, and on weekends—to handle situations that arise so, first and foremost, that would be in the area of communication.

2. *How does your mentoring help with your mentee's greatest challenge?*

It seems that helping a mentee gain perspective is one of the most important things a mentor can do. In order to do that, mentor comments suggest that building a trusting relationship with the mentee comes first. Then, the mentor can ask the mentee probing questions about challenges, needs, and successes. In this way, the mentee develops a wider perspective.

A mentor said:

I think the biggest way a mentor can help a mentee is by providing a relationship whose primary goal is to create perspective. By that I mean, if you think about a new principal coming into a building, who does that person have to talk to? Where is the collaborative team structure, the relationships where they can talk about the challenges, the needs or the successes, whatever it comes down to, getting perspective on what needs to happen?

Another mentor remarked:

Eventually, most administrators will create a cadre of people where they can brainstorm and get honest feedback about the challenges they face, but the mentor can provide a level of perspective. The most important things I think I did for my mentee were the questions that I asked. I think mentoring is about design, leadership that creates a community of designers. What designers do is notice things that other people do not see.

Habituation is things we have gotten used to, but often what we get used to and what we put up with are exactly the barriers that keep us from being able to resolve the problems that are in front of us. And so, the effectiveness of what I think great principals do is not figure out what the great leadership style is but what these principals notice and how they help other people notice what they have become fundamentally used to, and that is what I mean by perspective.

For example, my mentee noticed very early on that there was no professional development for her para-educators in her school. They did not necessarily feel part of the community, and they did not get the benefit of really understanding what their professional colleagues were working on, and so on.

My mentee noticed that. Then I asked her questions about that and what she might like to achieve and what she noticed about that and what was problematic to her. That then developed into a discussion she had with teachers, who then created a professional development program for the paras in her first year as principal. You can't fix what you don't notice. I think the essence of mentoring is helping give a principal greater perspective on what is going on, whether it is a success or a challenge.

3. *What is the most important thing your mentee is learning from you?*

Mentors suggest that helping their mentees learn to be patient with themselves allows them to reflect on their practice. Patience offers mentees time to think about how to decide and how that decision may play out. As one candid mentor wrote:

I have no idea. I hope a certain patience with oneself comes with the job. Young principals have so much pressure, and it does not all come in a single year. I hope my mentee is learning about the importance of reflection, of rethinking where one is. I hope that my mentee is learning to be patient with herself. Administrators can be very hard on themselves, shooting inward, particularly those who love children and love schools and take on the responsibilities of the world. I hope she is getting some personal perspective about the work.

Another mentor said, "Hopefully, patience and not having to make decisions immediately unless there is a physical or a safety issue."

And another commented:

I would want to be sure all mentors know not to start by giving advice. It is about asking questions and being adept at reading the needs of the mentee and not the needs of the mentor. That is something that was highly stressed in the NAESP (National Association of Elementary School Principals) training and in the VPA (Vermont Principals' Association) training. And so that I think was the big push that I had in my training.

4. *What could you not help your mentee with, and why not?*

As in question 2, the mentors suggest that their job is to empower their mentees to gain perspective. Mentors strive to help their mentees solve their problems without telling them what to do. Mentors would like their mentees to gain perspective on whatever they are trying to do in their practice.

"It is an interesting question," one mentor commented.

If I take it from the point of view that she was trying to do something and coming up with a right outcome, I would reject the premise of that question from the get-go, because that is not what basically I am here to do. I am not here to solve a problem for that person. My job as mentor is to empower my mentee so she can think and solve the problem.

When you step in, in any kind of a relationship, and you say you should do this, you really are sending a message that you are the expert and that you know what needs to happen here. And that the other person is not capable of handling this by himself or herself. I reject going down that road, and that is NOT what mentoring is about—and so I do not think there was anything that I could not help my mentee with, because if you believe getting perspective is right for whatever you are trying to do, then that is fundamentally a help.

5. *What suggestions would you have to enhance or improve the mentoring experience to reflect the Program/Initiative goals?*
    Vermont mentors would like the mentor training to be provided solely by the VPA. In this way, the training for retired principals is a required skill set.
    A mentor was quick to voice an opinion.

The Vermont mentor program is in alignment with the mentor goals, and there are five or six professional standards from the National Association about the role of mentors in creating trusting relationships and contributing to the field and staying informed.

One of the fundamental things that I learned early on was that I have forty-five years of experience and could mentor anyone, and the national association says that mentoring is a skill set and knowledge base, and I agree with it. Everybody should reflect on what it is, and I think that what Vermont wants is a cadre of skilled and trained mentors. Yet, some mentors are trained through the VPA and others are chosen by the superintendent, and I am unsure what the training is for such mentors. I think the mentor training should be via the VPA.

Another mentor concurred.

Vermont has put a lot of effort into mentoring since the legislature passed that first- and second-year principals should have a mentor and that districts have a responsibility to get them a mentor. But districts need to provide mentors who are VPA-trained. That understanding of what mentoring is and the required skill set needed should be made clearer.

Even though I am an experienced and trained mentor, in terms of my own professional development, I needed to go to professional conferences so I understand what principals are dealing with so I can have the greatest contextual sense of what is going on in the state and staying in the game. I think I could be more effective in my mentor role.

Another mentor added, "One suggestion I would have is to have as a required expectation is that the mentor listen to how the mentee handles difficult parents and board or committee members."

Tentative findings from the Vermont Mentoring study (2018) suggest that mentors often ask probing questions to help mentees reach their goals (Gimbel & Kefor, 2018). In this way, the mentors offer mentees time to ponder their thinking and their decisions by offering pertinent articles to read, web sites to visit, or virtual collaboration with other principals who have had similar issues. In so doing, the mentor is allowing the mentee to value multiple perspectives. The mentor creates the space for the mentee to look at issues from all stakeholders' perspectives. Hence, the mentee may not feel pressured to make a quick decision.

Chapter 6

The Massachusetts School Administrators Association Initiative

Limited or complicated access to time, training, and funding cause many school districts to hesitate at undertaking mentor initiatives. One way to combat the time constraint is by allowing mentors to use various modalities for conferring with their mentees as mentioned in chapter 3. The funding factor depends, among other things, on the availability of federal funds for administrator professional development as well as the local superintendent's allocation of resources and willingness to slow down principal turnover in his or her district, which impacts student achievement.

The Massachusetts School Administrators Association Mentoring Program for Administrators (MSAA) offers the following supports:

- Providing trained mentors who do not work or have not worked in the same district (with biographical information, if requested)
- Working with superintendents to develop goals, create implementation plans, and assess progress
- Continuing with monthly meetings on site, as well as communicating via phone or email whenever necessary
- Assisting administrators with building leadership, managerial, and super-visory skills
- Offering time and space for reflection on daily practice
- Submission of end-of-year reports on all meeting dates and educational topics (Massachusetts School Administrators Association [MSAA], 2019)

Since September 22, 2015, in order to obtain an unconditional professional license in Massachusetts, principals must participate in mentoring in the first year of their leadership position. All school districts are required to provide an induction program for all administrators, based upon the following standards provided by the Department of Elementary and Secondary Education, in 603 CMR7.13, Standards for Induction Programs for Administrators:

Standards. All induction programs shall meet the following requirements:

(a)

An orientation program for first-year administrators and all other administrators new to the district.

(b)

Assignment of first-year administrators to a trained mentor within the first two weeks of working.

(c)

Assignment of a support team that shall consist of, but not be limited to, the mentor and an administrator qualified to evaluate administrators.

(d)

Provision for adequate time for the mentor and beginning administrator to engage in professional conversations on learning and teaching as well as building leadership capacity within the school community and other appropriate mentoring activities.

(e)

Provision for adequate time and resources to learn how to use effective methods of personnel selection, supervision, and evaluation that are included in the Professional Standards for Administrators (603 CMR 7.10 (2)).

(3)

Additional Requirements. All induction programs shall submit an annual report to the Department that includes information on:

(a)

Program activities.

(b)

Number and complete list of beginning administrators served.

(c)

Number and complete list of trained mentors involved in the program.

(d)

Number of site-based visits made by mentors.

(e)

Number of hours that mentors and beginning administrators spent with each other.

(f)

Hiring and retention rates for first-year administrators.

(g)

Participant satisfaction.

(h)

Partnerships developed with other districts, professional associations, and institutions of higher education to support the administrator induction program.

Regulatory Authority:

M.G.L. c. 69, § 1B; c. 69, §§ 1J and 1K, as amended by St. 2010; c. 12, § 3; c. 71, §§ 38G, 38G ½; c. 71A, § 10; c. 76, § 19.

There is no required number of mentorship hours in the first year. Over the second and third years, however, principals must participate in fifty aggregate hours of additional mentoring. This may include emails, phone conversations, and other remote interactions.

MENTOR SELECTION

Each Massachusetts district determines how it will select mentors, with the stipulation that each mentor:

> must be an educator who has at least three full years of experience under an Initial or Professional License and who is trained to assist a beginning educator in the same professional role with his or her professional responsibilities and general school/district procedures. (CMR 7.02, p. 5)

According to the 2016 Massachusetts Department of Elementary and Secondary Education Statewide Induction and Mentoring Report, data suggest that some districts can choose mentors from a sizable pool of in-district applicants while other districts cannot; some districts choose to partner with another educational organization. The statewide organization, the MSAA, helps with identifying and training recently retired school principals to be mentors. The MSAA works with superintendents to facilitate a careful matching process based upon areas of expertise, goals, and type of setting (MSAA, 2018, Brochure).

THE MSAA TRAINING

Beyond state regulations, the purpose of the MSAA Mentor Program is to enhance the capacity of school leaders and to guide and direct sustained improvement of teaching and learning and the conditions under which they occur (MSAA, 2018, Brochure).

The MSAA mentoring program begins in the summer and runs for one school year. The trained mentor usually meets monthly, face to face with the new principal. The MSAA-trained mentor is also available as needed for phone consultations, email, or an online chat program. The MSAA's charge per program year is currently $2500, with 90 percent paid to the mentor. For superintendents, this is an insurance policy to help with principal retention. Districts can utilize funding sources like those available under the Vermont Initiative. The MSAA offers aspiring mentors a two-day intensive training program that includes the following topics:

- Entry Planning
- How to Set Goals

- How to Prepare for Mentor–Mentee Meetings
- Mentor Competencies
- Norms of Collaboration
- How to build trust
- How to offer feedback
- The Massachusetts Standards for Administrators
- How to Reflect on Practice

MASSACHUSETTS VOICES: MENTOR TRAINING FEEDBACK

After the two-day Massachusetts School Administrators' Association mentor training, trainees have an opportunity to offer feedback on the session. Below are some of the questions from the workshop evaluation form (MSAA, January, 2019, Conference) and respective comments; from the comments one can easily parse out some of the session content:

1. *Identify one concept in the workshop that you found particularly pertinent to your position. What is your current thinking about this?*
   - "Sharing ideas and thoughts; getting multiple perspectives and hearing about other's experiences"
   - "Risk-taking levels related to trust"
   - "Wealth of knowledge shared by participants/colleagues. Also, establishing networking relationships"
   - "How to discuss the role of the mentor with the mentee"
   - "Discussions about the articles we read"
   - "Trust discussion"
   - "Relationships discussion"
   - "Entry plan questioning"
   - "Good to network with others"
   - "Developing a supportive and trusting relationship"
   - "Understanding the culture of the school; mentoring checklists"
2. *What are the one or two things that you will go back and pursue to move yourself forward and/or your school forward?*
   - "Recommit to the power of being a good listener and commit to that as a mentor"
   - "In addition to one-on-one mentoring conversations, ask more about how classes and faculty meetings are going"
   - "Reread the articles"

- "Entry plan, goal-setting, agenda"
- "Develop a list of topics and scenarios"
- "Be mindful of the stages of the mentor relationship and how those stages impact change"
- "Cut out the 'culture of nice'; direct feedback builds trust"

3. *What were the most helpful parts of the workshop?*
    - "The readings got us thinking and sharing"
    - "Group work"
    - "Open discussion about articles"
    - "Facilitator allowed for conversations and sharing"
    - "How having conversations with mentee should occur"
    - "Small, interactive conversations were extremely helpful"
    - "Discussion, sharing of articles, scenarios"
    - "Discussion as a cohort"
    - "Discussion in small groups"
    - "Sharing perspectives and scenarios with the role the mentor should play"
    - "Conversations, articles, group interaction, checklists"

MENTORING AT THE HALF-WAY MARK
(MSAA, 2019)

The MSAA mentor cohort meets halfway through the first year of mentoring. At the winter 2019 meeting, mentors discussed their successes and challenges. Here are some of their comments:

Mentor A: "The mentee I am with had to let someone go within ninety days. She is working with two new assistant principals. She has a sense of leadership. Most of the mentoring is about trust and building relationships. We work on meeting goals and how they fit with the superintendent, but I have not yet met the superintendent."

Mentor B: "This is my first go-round. I have a principal in elementary school, and she loves getting a different perspective. An assistant principal and the principal do not see eye to eye. I need to think about how to tell the principal to bide her time and then counsel her to move on."

Mentor C: I like my mentee. I am mentoring a principal who is now in a school that has grades four through seven. It was grades four through five. This is his second year; he was interim and now he is staying, as people heard him say if he likes it, he will stay. But the fourth and fifth grade teachers liked the previous person who is not there. So, we are working on culture. My mentee really is a middle-school person. He emails me and calls me, as he is not familiar with grades four and five. I suggested using the Massachusetts School Administrators Association (MSAA) school culture survey.

Mentor D: "I start our meetings with, 'So what are the great things going on? And what else?' My mentee says things are 20 percent problem and 80 percent great. So, I told her, 'Just realize that you have only been a six-month principal. Reflect on what you are doing well.'"

Mentor E: I love the mentoring, and I have two new principals in different districts. I suggested we use an online app to communicate. Yesterday one of my mentees got on the app to describe a problem. It is sometimes easier to do it on the app because this gave her time to do research and to get an article and to sleep on it and think it through. We have collaborative time, and we keep confidentiality in our relationship and like collaborating. Our meetings are scheduled when we have time, and we go to one or the other person's school. Networking is still an issue, and the two superintendents have not been able to get out into the schools. The issue of relating with assistant principals is a sensitive issue. I try to ask what is successful so I can build up their confidence and competence.

Mentor E continued: This is a great experience. I am mentoring two people: a Pre-K–1 principal and a middle school principal not new to being principal, but new to the community. There is a "challenge" of having a new superintendent. I wish I had more contact with the superintendent.

I have two different principals who are grappling with how different the community is from their past ones, and both of the principals are trying to understand the lay of the land. They want to focus on the challenges. The middle school principal has a long-term sub in Spanish who is working with a veteran teacher, and the principal is struggling. The two teachers cannot be in the same room. Parents are worried about the long-term sub. And for the other Pre-K–1 principal, the school secretary retired, and the new principal is affected by this. The middle school principal has also had personal challenges (a tree fell on his house, and he is living in a trailer).

What does the superintendent want from the two teachers of Spanish? The middle school principal wants to know what the superintendent wants for the community. I spoke to the superintendent, and that helped her.

Mentor F: I am mentoring one new principal and one new vice-principal in the same school, and they work together well. They have different needs and personalities; one is open to different suggestions and is willing to learn and asks about personnel issues. But I want to know how to help mentees "beyond the immediate stuff." A lot of reassurance is important for the mentees.

Some of the things my mentees want to do is work on schedules and then process decision-making.

Mentor G: I am mentoring four elementary principals. One is new, and two are new assistant principals to be split between two schools. Relationships are an issue between these folks. One of the goals is to hire two more assistant principals but structured over a two-year period. It is a well-thought-out process. The new principal came into a difficult situation with a new assistant principal, and now she is a new principal in a school where there was no assistant principal before. We are working through all of this.

Over the summer, I met with two of them. I meet monthly with each triad and then with all six, and I try to help the superintendent to present funding for more assistant principals. The organizational structure is the issue. Sometimes I watch the principals to see their actions, and I wonder if it is their personalities that are challenging.

THE FACILITATOR ASKED: WHAT CAUGHT YOU OFF GUARD?

Mentor G: "Hard to believe there are dysfunctional districts in this day and age."
Mentor H: "How far behind they are in the basic things—lack of culture and communication. Each school is an island unto itself."
Mentor I: "Range of age. They don't know what they don't know."

THE FACILITATOR ASKED: WHAT COULD WE ADD IN THE TRAINING WE PROVIDED?

Mentor J: "More about the relationship of the principal to the superintendent. It would be helpful to remind the principal to meet with their superintendents early on."
Mentor K: "I was invited in the summer to meet with the administrative team in August, which was a good idea for me to become acquainted with them before the school year began."
Mentor L: "Summer is important to work on the mentor–mentee relationship."

Mentor M: "Talking to the superintendent is valuable but keeping confidence in the mentor–mentee relationship is important."

Mentor N: "I met with the superintendent early on, and then in December I sent an email to him to update him on the mentor relationship midway through the program."

ONE MENTOR ASKED IF OTHERS HAD COME UP WITH WAYS TO REPORT ON THE MENTOR YEAR TO THE DISTRICT?

Mentor A: "I give dates and times and a log to show the superintendent. Some mentees use logs as evidence of professional practice."

Mentor B: "I do likewise."

Mentor C: "I use Google Docs to do this."

Mentor D: "I will set up Google Docs for us to dump articles of interest to all of us."

We will discuss key takeaways from the Vermont and Massachusetts programs in the next chapters.

Chapter 7

Lessons from the 2020 Massachusetts Mentor Survey

In lieu of its annual face-to-face meeting of mentors, in March 2020, during the COVID-19 pandemic when social distancing was mandated, the Massachusetts School Administrators Association (MSAA) sent out a brief questionnaire to mentors to see how their relationships were going with the new principals they were mentoring.

The four questions posed to mentors were:

- What are your thoughts up to March 1, 2020?
- What caught you off guard?
- Did anything surprise you about the new principals?
- What could we add to the training we provided?

The collection of annualized data on the mentoring program is an important part of the process of continuous program improvement that the MSAA has set for itself, and responses to the 2020 survey were instructive. By mid-year, mentors have plenty of experiences and perspectives to share, and data from the survey suggests that issues affecting new principals, as seen by mentors, fall into several categories. These include:

- Meeting superintendents' expectations
- Listening and being listened to
- Handling issues not directly related to instructional leadership
- Balancing work and life
- Working with teachers and staff

- Handling union issues
- Mentoring the same mentee beyond Year One

MEETING SUPERINTENDENTS' EXPECTATIONS

A good working relationship with the district superintendent's office is key to a successful principalship, especially in its early years. One mentor wrote in the 2020 survey that the superintendent in her mentee's district wanted the new principal/mentee to become more familiar with the special education laws in Massachusetts and with special education issues in his school.

Several other mentors replied that superintendents had specific things they wanted their mentees to focus on so that they would be successful in their respective schools. Some of the superintendents' demands pertained to building relationships and school cultures and climates. In fact, in one school district, the mentor explained that the principal turnover was high, and the superintendent wanted the new principal to succeed in order to avoid having to hire another principal.

Mentors, who meet with mentees' superintendents as part of the MSAA program, reported that "Each superintendent made it very clear that they wanted the administrator to be successful and offered support and assistance." Another mentor observed,

I will say that up until now, we have some successes and some not-so-successful situations. The year started off smoothly. The superintendent asked me to help with the school culture and climate, especially the principal's relationship with staff.

We discussed ideas to build the relationship with staff starting with faculty meetings such as celebrating successes, good news, acknowledgments, etc. We worked on school-wide culture-building activities with monthly themes such as the Kindness Tree and a school-wide discipline policy where the teachers are working together to develop a pre-office referral form.

Regarding mentors working with superintendents, another mentor commented, "I think touching base with the superintendents in September, January and June helps. The first meeting is to hear their concerns, and the January meeting is to be sure they feel everything is going well. The final meeting helps show the work you have accomplished and the growth the administrator has made."

LISTENING AND BEING LISTENED TO

Mentors also wrote of the importance of listening hard and carefully to their mentees until the relationship is established and trust is evident. One mentor commented, "My thoughts up to March 1 were that we were just hitting our stride, and my mentee was asking more for my help and sharing more. He asked for help on scheduling, and we worked for over an hour. I felt the trust was really starting to happen."

"I think mentoring new administrators is a great idea," noted a mentor, "and it seems like each one uses a mentor differently. Some just like to talk and have another person listen and acknowledge their work, while others look for advice and others like to show off their schools and have someone to acknowledge their hard work."

Another mentor wrote that he was "surprised by how long it took to get to the trust level. My principal is somewhat of an introvert and was reluctant to open up with his true thoughts and feelings until around late January, when he felt his superintendent abandoned him on a discipline issue."

One mentor summed up many of the comments by saying, "I think every mentor's situation is different. Being a good listener is the best advice—how to listen and not just give advice and look like a 'know-it-all.' I also feel it is important to let the administrator know how central administration feels about them and work toward the two of them having a strong bond and good professional relationship."

HANDLING ISSUES NOT DIRECTLY RELATED TO INSTRUCTIONAL LEADERSHIP

What else surprised new principals? "The new principal was somewhat surprised by the amount of time that needed to be devoted to 'non-educational issues' during the school day," wrote one mentor, while another believes that "The challenge for the principals is that they are relatively new as well and so academic, behavioral, and social and emotional programs are evolving and being initiated differently at all levels."

BALANCING WORK AND LIFE

Finding ways to maintain a healthy balance between work and personal life is an ongoing issue for principals. One mentor noted that "the role of the principal continues to evolve into a 24/7 job. The continued need is for the mentee to understand the importance of the balance between the school job and family life." Another observed that "balancing school and life is an enormous challenge for mentees."

WORKING WITH TEACHERS AND STAFF

Schools, with all their stakeholder groups considered, are relatively large organizations requiring skilled leadership and nuanced decisions. Things can proceed relatively calmly, as one mentor wrote: "The district is currently working on addressing district/school climate as it relates to educators. Mentoring administrators at all three levels has enabled me to have a more accurate global view of the system, which has led to rich conversation and further support for the administrators."

But mistakes can be costly, making the mentor's role even more valuable. A mentor reported:

> What surprised me the most is how quickly the [mentee] principal reacts to situations before thinking them through. For example, at an IST meeting, a teacher asked her a question about sharing an aide, and she immediately said no. She is very defensive and does not like it when a teacher questions her decision. We discussed responding with "Let me think about it" or "Let's discuss it at our next faculty meeting." I am trying to help her delegate a little more and let the staff be a part of the decision-making. In this area, she is improving.

HANDLING UNION ISSUES

The sometimes-complicated relationship between school administrators and teachers' unions also surfaced as an area requiring mentorship. "What caught me [as a mentor] off guard are the union issues against the principal that have popped up," wrote one mentor. "For example, the principal hired a new technology teacher, and the union does not like the schedule that the principal arranged, so the union president, who happens to be in the building, filed a grievance. Another grievance was filed over the schedule of the teacher assistants. It seems an assistant was asked to cover for a teacher who was late and then did not show up for the entire day, so the union president filed another grievance."

Most mentors are experienced with working with teachers' unions, and a new principal who faces challenges relating to the conditions of unionized employees' work may need extra support in this area. A mentor observed, "Union resistance is different at different levels, which has prevented some levels from initiating change sooner."

A third mentor summed up the challenges of a mentee's year: "The not-so-successful situations have to do with the teachers' union and several union officers who are members of the staff."

MENTORING THE SAME MENTEE BEYOND YEAR ONE

Regarding trust-building, other mentors indicated that mentoring the same principal for a second year allows for more dialogue: "A valuable program for new principals who need the ability to discuss issues that many times are not part of their professional training. This is my second year with my mentee, and I was surprised by the request for another year. When I asked 'why' he indicated that it was the professional dialogue and the ability to discuss issues with a person not associated with the district. "

Another mentor observed that "I notice that having a mentor for more than one year is also helpful, and after building a bond and a trust, the administrator really starts opening up and listening to their mentors and using them to be productive."

A third mentor commented that "mentoring people for two years has given us an opportunity to dig deep. I am now very familiar with the school and have built a deep, trusting relationship. This year has focused on the goals for the school. It is very important for mentors to put their items at the top of our agenda so that we can focus on the issues of the day, along with the longer-term goals."

RECOMMENDATIONS FOR FUTURE TRAINING

Mentors' replies to the final question about what could be provided in future MSAA Mentor Trainings are instructive for anyone planning to develop a mentor training program. Here are some responses:

"More emphasis placed on dealing with crisis management during the school day."

"I think it would be nice to host an event with all of the mentees and mentors just to expand their network."

"Our training was one and half days. If we had a full second day, we would have time to process more—for example, active listening, questioning, and feedback need processing in order to become more internalized for each mentor. This could be done with triad experiences: one person is mentee, one is mentor, and the third is the observer."

> I think there could be more focus on the additional challenge the new principal has when he or she is not new to the role but new to the school and community. Assumptions may be made by the principal and/or the stakeholders that may or may not be true and that can cause more frustration or misunderstanding because the person has been a principal somewhere else. I think it would be helpful to suggest to the mentors in these situations that they focus on identifying possible areas that could be land mines if the principal and superintendent aren't explicit about goals and transition needs.

"I would recommend a focus on strategies to support the well-being of the new administrator, to help them learn to delegate and empower others so that they do not feel overwhelmed by all the demands and needs of others. This year I witnessed a lot of teachers and staff who try to put all problems and issues on the back of the principal."

"In regard to what could be added to the training, I benefited from the training I received because there were administrators who were participating in the training that had already been mentoring. I found that their sharing their experiences to be very worthwhile."

In the next chapters we will step back to consider the deeper lessons to be learned from the Vermont and Massachusetts programs.

Chapter 8

Making Sense of Mentor Voices from Vermont and Massachusetts

There are clear commonalities between the mentor voices from Vermont, expressed in interview questions about the mentor-mentee relationship, and the mentor voices from Massachusetts, obtained from the 2019 mid-year mentoring meeting and the 2020 survey. Both mentor groups discuss trust, relationship-building, and valuing different perspectives as important focal points in their mentor-mentee relationships.

Vermont mentors realize that helping principals prepare for critically observing classes and for potentially difficult meetings and conversations requires a great deal of time, while Massachusetts mentors point out that principals' dealings with superintendents can require intensive dialogue. Massachusetts superintendents would like to discuss which initiatives the new principal should undertake and when.

These superintendents appreciate the opportunity to meet with mentors for interactive conversations and, time permitting, would appreciate additional meetings. Both Vermont and Massachusetts mentor groups see a need for more continuous "professional mentor development," especially around trust, the sharing of different perspectives, and building relations.

TAKEAWAYS FROM BOTH PROGRAMS

Both the Vermont and Massachusetts principal mentorship programs share a focus on several key areas:

Entry Planning. Perhaps no period in a principal's tenure is as important as the first days, weeks, and months. It is helpful to work with a mentor on such questions as how, to whom, and when a new principal introduces himself or herself to a new school and how best to present key constituencies—families, students, teachers, the community at large—with the new principal's persona and professional hopes for the school in the context of district and state strategic priorities. Also important is the development of strategies for building understanding of and engagement with this work.

Professional Standards. Each state has its own professional standards by which a principal must live and work and against which they will be evaluated. It is important, then, that the new principal understands these standards not only as an articulated framework for evaluation but as the overarching, guiding rubric for their professional actions and on which their decisions must be based.

Reflection. Axiomatic as it may be in educational circles that reflection and habits of reflective practice are important, it is equally axiomatic that the exigencies of the professional life of high-level school administrators tend to preclude such reflection. That the Vermont and Massachusetts training programs focus on reflection as a key professional tool reminds us that new principals need to be shown (and perhaps trained in) both the art of reflection and the need to prioritize reflection in their professional lives and practice.

Norms of Collaboration. Building cultures of collaborative practice can look very different depending on one's position in a school hierarchy. Helping new principals learn the skills of leading collaborative efforts and enlisting the support and positive participation of others—including not just multiple school-level constituencies but also district-level teams and even boards—is key to any principal's success. These skills can and should be taught to and learned, often framed by real day-to-day issues, by new principals.

Mentor Competencies. Mentors have their own learning needs, and it should come as no surprise that these successful state-mandated programs include specific instruction in the tools and dispositions required for effective mentoring. Mentor trainees, volunteers for the most part, have a strong desire to help and support new principals, but programs must offer specific tutelage on the most effective ways and means of turning good intentions into effective action.

OTHER AREAS IN NEED OF GREATER ATTENTION

The de-briefs with mentors revealed several other areas not only for further development on the mentoring front, but that might also require further attention from schools of education and other preparatory and professional development programs for school administrators. These include greater attention to issues such as laws and regulations respecting special education, to issues of diversity, equity, and inclusion, and to working effectively with unionized teacher bodies.

And clearly, the relationship between principal and superintendent has taken on increasing complexity in recent years, and supporting new principals and principals-to-be develop skills in and strategies for working with superintendents to understand district priorities and cultures must be a priority for all concerned with principal development.

WHY MENTORING IS NEEDED

Principals are responsible for creating the culture, the systems, and instructional conditions necessary for all children to achieve at high levels in an economic and social context that is complex, challenging and fraught with inequity for children and families. Nationally, one in four principals remain in place in a school over a five-year period, with 20 percent of new urban principals leaving the profession within two years. (RAND Corporation, 2012)

Over time, mentoring novice principals can help with principal retention, creating greater stability in schools. The NASSP/LPI Research Brief (Levin & Bradley, 2019) points out that better prepared principals who have had mentors or internships are less stressed and stay longer, even if they are in high-need schools. "The paucity of quality mentoring programs is retarding states' efforts to ensure that every student attends a school where strong leadership results in high academic performance" (Wallace Foundation, 2007, SREB, p. 5).

The idea of providing a new leader in any profession an experienced guide and role model is not a new idea. In many fields this notion has gained wide acceptance. To reduce teacher attrition in public education, for example, some forms of mentoring were introduced in schools in the 1980s (Wallace Foundation, 2007); in independent schools, mentoring for teachers new to a school or to the profession has been common for several decades. For novice principals, however, only recently have some states and some school districts offered mentoring support to their new school principals.

As we discussed in the Introduction, the principalship is more demanding than ever. New principals need to learn names and faces of a large community of stakeholders, including teachers, staff, students, district administrators, parents, school board, and members of the community-at-large. They also need to learn the politics of the district. They must learn on the job, because so much occurs daily in their world. The pace of the principalship is so fast that new principals do not have time to reflect on what they may be learning. Under scrutiny, any misstep a new principal makes may have an impact much larger than anticipated.

Yet, despite the need for principal mentoring programs, it seems that some challenges may be slowing down the adoption of principal mentoring programs. Such factors may include mentor selection and training, the establishment of appropriate criteria for matching mentors and new principals, compensation of mentors, funding for mentor programs, and gauging the subject matter for mentoring to meet the needs of each new principal, the district goals, and the state standards (p. 5). Moreover, data on how mentoring helps retain principals seems to be anecdotal and subjective, aimed primarily at describing the satisfaction levels in mentor-mentee relationships rather than on specific aspects of program efficacy.

Lack of time, training, and funding are factors that impede many school districts from mentor initiatives. As discussed in chapter 3, one way to combat the time constraint is by allowing mentors to employ various modalities for conferring with their mentees. The funding factor depends on federal funds for professional development for administrators and the local superintendent's willingness to slow down principal turnover in his or her district by allocating resources for principal mentoring.

Regarding training, some mentoring programs rely on active principals as mentors, rather than retired principals who have time as well as the expertise to devote to mentoring and to being trained. Principals' associations, such as the VPA in Vermont and the MSAA in Massachusetts, offer training to retired, experienced school leaders from both independent and public schools.

WHY PRINCIPAL INDUCTION

Smith & Piele (2006) describe the passage of new principals from the survival phase to the initial period to the professional actualization phase, wherein they collaborate with teachers to advance an agenda. This suggests that new principals need support during the early stages in order to arrive at the actualization stage. Induction by mentoring can help new principals devise their first-year goals and how to achieve them.

Without adequate development programs, such as mentoring, new principals have a much smaller likelihood of a strong start to their careers. The first two years of a principal's tenure are critical, as that is when principals decide whether the job is overwhelming and whether they should stay or leave. Leadership stability is essential for school improvement, and new principals need to feel supported in their job (Gimbel & Kefor, 2018, p. 2).

It seems that states and districts tend to overlook support for school leaders once they are in the "seat" (Rowland, 2017). As was mentioned in chapters 3 and 4, only twenty states required any form of professional support for new principals (Gimbel & Kefor, 2018, p. 4; Goldrick, 2016). (There does not seem to be more current data on this form of professional development for new principals.)

Even though there is a need for principal mentoring, it has not often been the subject of rigorous research, and there is not yet a well-developed theoretical foundation (Smith & Piele, 2006, p. 118). Moreover, clear trends in mentoring programs are not apparent. There are programs that only pair a new principal with an experienced peer, and then let them work out their relationship on their own (p. 118). As we have suggested, new principals need trained mentors.

The NYC Leadership Academy (2019), a proponent of mentoring programs to strengthen new principals' performance and help with their retention, conducted a review of the literature. Through the literature review and academy members' own experiences in the field, they "identified seven effective practices for the induction and onboarding of new principals" (NYC Leadership Brief, 2019). These are their identified practices:

1. Deliver a high-quality summer induction program prior to the first year of the principalship.
2. Anchor the program design and assessment in leadership performance standards.
3. Structure opportunities for collaboration and socialization.
4. Engage principals in authentic, experiential leadership experiences to enable them to apply newly acquired knowledge and skills in meaningful ways (Bloom et al., 2005).
5. Deliver individual coaching or mentoring.
6. Embed opportunities for problem-based learning.
7. Provide ongoing professional development and support.

CONSIDERATIONS FOR MENTORING PROGRAM DEVELOPMENT

Given the need for mentoring and the benefits of mentoring, what should be considered in developing a mentoring program? In order to begin, several questions need to be considered.

Who will plan the program? How will mentors be selected and trained? How will mentors and mentees be matched? How will the program be evaluated? (Smith & Piele, 2006).

In 2016, the Massachusetts Department of Elementary and Secondary Education surveyed school districts statewide about their induction and mentoring programs. Results suggest that new principals need support in the following areas: communication skills, managing conflict, data-driven decision-making, providing feedback to teachers, and evaluation. These areas are integrated into the MSAA mentoring program.

The Washington State Association of School Principals (2016) also devised a list of considerations for program development. Their areas of consideration include:

Model identification: What model for principal mentorship will best serve our district needs?

Mentor Selection: What criteria will be used to select mentors?

Training of Mentors: How will we support the development of mentors so that they understand and support the development of new principals?

Training for Mentees/New Principals: How will the professional development needs of new principals be met?

BEST PRACTICES

The Wallace Foundation report (2007) sums up the most important considerations when putting a principal mentoring program in place:

- Provide at least one year of support
- Require high-quality training
- Provide funding for training, stipends and meaningful induction
- Gather data about efficacy
- Maintain clear goals for new principals to lead change

Chapter 9

Common Challenges of First-Year Principals

Although each school differs in staff, student, and community composition, there are some common challenges facing first-year principals. In discussions of the struggles of their mentee principals, Vermont and Massachusetts mentors regularly cite establishing trust, developing effective communication strategies, building relationships in the school and district, and maintaining a healthy work–life balance.

TRUST

As seen in Figure 9.1, communication, relationships/collaboration, and work–life balance emanate from trust. Therefore, it is important for the new principal to start working on building trust as soon as possible. "Literature from the 1990s implies that trust rests on the ability of the principal to promote relationships with teachers. The challenge of leadership in schools is to build a trusting relationship between leader and follower" (Gimbel, 2003, p. 54). As mentioned in chapter 2, trust is the foundation on which the principal can build and sustain one-to-one relationships.

In chapter 7, Massachusetts mentors mentioned that maintaining a healthy balance between work and the personal lives of their mentees was an issue. A school principal "needs to be able to count on teachers to help implement policies that he or she holds to be important" (p. 3). In a study conducted by one of the authors, both survey and interview data suggest that there are common elements of trust-building exhibited by effective principals. These

Figure 9.1   The Essential Elements of Trust in School Leadership. (Cherkowski & Walker, 2020)

trust-promoting leader practices, agreed upon by both teacher and principal respondents, can be sorted into supportive and communicative principal behaviors (Gimbel, 2003, p. 54).

Effective supportive principal behaviors include:

- Maintaining confidentiality
- Treating all teachers fairly
- Being consistently responsive
- Soliciting input from teachers
- Recognizing good work
- Being considerate and caring about teachers' personal lives
- Being willing to admit mistakes
- Leading collegially

Effective communicative principal behaviors include:

- Confronting conflict and trying to resolve it
- Providing timely, accurate information
- Articulating goals and expectations

- Practicing empathic, active listening
- Sharing decision-making
- Being visible for informal dialogue

COMMUNICATION

Too many school leaders have learned the hard way, that, as George Bernard Shaw once observed, the single biggest problem in communication is the illusion that is has taken place (Medium, 2019, "What's Most Important" section, para. 1). Because something has been said or written does not mean that it has been heard or read or that the content of a message has been understood or internalized for action.

Being an effective communicator is one of the new principal's greatest challenges. Conflict can result from miscommunication and misinformation (Gimbel & Leana, 2013). Inadequate communication between teachers and their evaluators is a huge stumbling block (p. 17). New principals need to know what communicative behaviors inspire trust and build relationships.

Effective communicative behaviors for principals not only contribute to principal–teacher trust, they are also critical to every aspect of a principal's practice. One of the pitfalls for a new leader is an inability to initiate difficult conversations. Often, new school principals want to be a "nice leader," and so they avoid contentious issues, such as performance evaluations, addressing grievances, or dealing with a disgruntled teacher or staff member.

This avoidance, because it soon becomes obvious, does not enhance the new principal's relationships with teachers, who need to feel that their administration is actively engaged in essential work and for whom communication is the pathway toward collaboration and common purpose. It is important for the principal to communicate, to be present in ongoing discussions, and to clarify expectations to avoid teacher frustration and conflict (Gimbel & Leana, 2013, p. 13).

An apparent absence of such interpersonal skills as empathy, the ability to resolve conflicts, and the ability to work collaboratively are among the more frequent reasons principal contracts are not renewed (Gimbel, 2003). Empathy has been described as the ability to put oneself in another person's shoes and to experience how they feel in their shoes (Quy, 2019), and empathetic, active listening is a communicative behavior that builds trust.

By listening with care, a new school principal can build rapport with teachers so that can in turn enable supportive development. Empathy also involves sensing whether a message has been conveyed by understanding and identifying with the emotions of the audience. This helps when there is a conflict, because the new principal can understand the other party's perspectives and needs. If there is a conflict, empathy allows the school leader to work more easily toward a win–win solution.

RELATIONSHIP BUILDING AND COLLABORATION

The more information teachers have about what is expected of them in their work, the more effective they become. It is up to new principals to share information and openly discuss successes, changes, and failures. Such communication fosters transparency and a culture of collaboration (Kohm & Nance, 2009). New principals are challenged to build cultural norms that support the faculty working together. They can do this by the supportive and communicative behaviors cited above.

Part of this process involves sharing decision-making. Principals need to pay attention to how information is disseminated. Communicative behaviors that support a collaborative culture include being sure that accurate, timely information reaches all teachers, forestalling the spread of rumors and misinformation. Involving teachers in solving problems and sharing ideas acknowledges and builds on their professionalism and creates a transparent culture, conducive to collaboration.

New principals are challenged to work with teachers on setting realistic goals together. Without a collaborative culture, the new principal may not be able to achieve goals the superintendent wants him or her to accomplish. Mutually developed goals allow the principal to be the person who establishes the conditions for goal attainment.

This sharing of information and expectations extends to the building of positive relationships between the principal and the superintendent, as well. Principals must expect transparency from district officers, and they must also be clear in their understanding of district goals and expectations. In return, principals need to be open and direct in communicating the challenges they face in their own buildings as part of communicating their expectation of support but also to build a lasting, collaborative relationship with the superintendent and their office.

WORK–LIFE BALANCE

In the 2020 National Association of Secondary School Principals (NASSP) survey, over 50 percent of principals reported spending at least sixty hours a week on school-related activities. In another NASSP survey of first- and second-year principals, 44 percent of respondents cited time management as their top challenge (Goode & Shinkle, 2020). And in April 2020 at a virtual MSAA mentor meeting, mentors reported that work–life balance was a challenge for their mentees.

As mentioned in chapter 3, the job of a new principal can be overwhelming. New principals can be overcome with information and communication technology, issues related to the many kinds of student diversity, an increase in accountability, performing teacher evaluations, and other initiatives aimed at improving student outcomes. There is pressure to meet the goals the superintendent has articulated, and principals need time simply to build relationships and trust that can lead to a culture of shared leadership. And time is needed to attend to fiscal and operational demands (Ontario Principals Council, 2017).

This increase in work intensity can impair the well-being of the new principal, which can lead to problems for the school community as it seeks the attention and engagement of its leader. Finding what issues to take on first and how to tackle them is a challenge for the principal, for whom superhuman efforts and their own expectations of "getting it all done" can also lead to feelings of frustration, guilt, and inadequacy—which in turn have consequences both for schools and for principals and their personal lives.

The problem of finding the "right" work–life balance is often identified by new principals themselves. With the help of effective mentors, principals can set about building relationships and trust by developing the skills identified throughout this book. Armed with skills in communication and supportiveness, new principals can build cultures of collaboration and trust. In such cultures, where shared purposes and mutual respect are understood, principals, rather than taking on every task in isolation, can confidently delegate responsibilities to their teachers and staff—allowing the principals time to figure out not only what needs to be done and when but also how to pursue personal interests and find satisfaction into their own lives.

IN CONCLUSION

Observing growing levels of stress and burnout in K–12 Schools, two Canadian professors put together a fact sheet on "Workplace Well-Being in K–12 Schools" (see Figure 9.1). Drs. Cherkowski & Walker (2020) propose that compassion, trust, and hope will help school communities flourish.

More specifically for school leaders, they suggest a "leadership mindset" that can create a culture that encourages all staff to identify ways that their individual work contributes to the larger, shared goals of the school community. The challenge for new principals is to create trust via positive relationships and collaboration, fostering a sense of shared leadership and common purpose and community well-being.

Facing growing levels of stress and burnout, K-12 staff require a supportive workplace that encourages them to find ways to "flourish" within their school community. While flourishing may look different to staff members depending on what makes them personally feel most valued and connected to their work, a flourishing school environment generally has three main components:

1. Subjective Well-Being: positive emotions, positive relationships, and a sense of making a difference are all aspects that contribute to a staff member's sense of flourishing.

2. Adaptive Community: an environment where staff are encouraged to communicate openly with colleagues, be creative, and resolve team conflicts when they arise.

3. Leaderful Mindsets: staff are able to identify ways that their work contributes to the larger, shared goals of the school community, which provides a greater sense of ownership, engagement, and shared leadership.

Along with these components, staff in flourishing school communities generally demonstrate key "professional characteristics," including:

1. Compassion: noticing and wanting to help ease the stress of others, and are aware of how their thoughts and actions impact their colleagues.

2. Trust: having the support and autonomy to take creative risks and innovate, which is reflective of having positive relationships with colleagues.

3. Hope: striving to improve the school environment as a whole-school community by recognizing both strengths and challenges, while building a shared vision for improvement.

Figure 9.2   Conceptual Model for Flourishing In Schools. (Cherkowski & Walker, 2020)

Chapter 10

First-Year Challenges and the Mentoring Process

As discussed previously, the challenges facing a new principal can be over-whelming. Having a trusted mentor who has been in the position before and who can be an unbiased listener helps the new principal lessen the stress of the job. But what can mentors do to help a new principal sort the issues he or she faces and help build leadership confidence?

Mentors in Massachusetts and Vermont are trained to help their mentees with many of their first-year challenges. These mentors also work with super-intendents to help the mentee develop goals and create an implementation plan. By facilitating in-depth discussions on how to build trusting relation-ships in the school and in the district and on ways to create a culture of col-legiality, mentors point to actions that will assist the new principals in their practice. The precise nature of these actions must be based upon the context of the school community and the expectations of the superintendent.

HOW MENTORS HELP MENTEES WITH FIRST-YEAR CHALLENGES

Guided by our discussions with Vermont and Massachusetts mentors and the work of Weingartner (2009), we offer some ways that mentors can assist their mentees in meeting their first-year challenges.

1. Mentors need to begin the relationship with a low-key approach. Since mentors are experienced principals, they could be intimidating if they

present themselves too forcefully. The mentor needs to act first as a neutral sounding board as issues arise in leadership practice.

2. Always be positive and supportive. For the mentee to build self-esteem, even while asking for advice, it is important for the mentor to provide the rationale and context behind any questions the mentors pose about the mentee's practice. In this way, the mentee may accept the mentor's suggestions more readily.

3. Celebrate being the mentee. Most new principals will feel pleased with their new leadership positions, which have been achieved by hard work and training. As such, the mentor's initial contact with the mentee should include some congratulatory gesture; perhaps a card or a plant. In this way, the mentor is setting the tone for a positive, generous relationship.

4. Let the mentee drive how much help the mentor can be. The mentor's success depends upon maintaining readiness and openness to understanding the mentee's learning curve. Advice to the mentee needs to come at the right time; if the mentee is not ready to receive the advice, it won't be understood or useful to the mentee.

5. Be willing to back off or admit uncertainty. The mentor will make some mistakes in timing even if their ideas or suggestions may be very good. The mentor should ask for feedback when that happens and learn from it. It is best not to create an impression of pushiness or to be dogmatic, as these mannerisms will disincline the mentee from accepting whatever suggestion is made.

6. Don't take rejection of ideas personally; rejection could be a matter of readiness. Perhaps the mentee was not at the place on their personal learning curve to accept the suggestion.

7. Continually reinforce the confidential nature of the relationship; it is extremely important for the mentee to know that conversations are confidential. Conversations that take place in an atmosphere of candor and security allow for deeper sharing and signal a deepening relationship and trust. The mentor must earn that trust.

8. Recognize the need for the mentee to have personal time outside of school. Be sure the mentee has some time for personal life where s/he does not need to think about the issues and challenges of leading discussed in the mentorship.

9. Be there for the mentee, but frame the limitations of the role. It is important for the mentee to understand that the mentor is there to support the mentee, but not to help be a "silent partner" in running the school.

10. Maintain confidentiality in discussing the mentee with administrators. It is best to remain protective and circumspect regarding private aspects of mentorship in the mentor's conversations with the superintendent or evaluator. The mentee should be present for and part of any discussion that requires exploration of matters the mentee might regard as sensitive.

11. Motivate mentees to think for themselves. The goal of mentorship is to help new principals develop the skills and confidence for independent leadership and decision-making. Reflective practice is a key tool in any part of education, and the mentor should pose questions that promote reflection. This will prompt the mentee to think deeply about and consider multiple aspects of any decision there is to be made rather than rushing to judgment.

12. Mentors can also gain from the mentoring experience. Sometimes new principals come to their positions with a lot of creativity and enthusiasm. Mentors themselves need to be open to learning new ways of approaching leadership challenges and practices.

WHAT IS NOT PART OF THE MENTORING PROCESS?

There are certain mentor activities that are not part of the mentoring process. Here are what the Vermont Principals' Association suggests are *not* part of the mentoring services, with our description of each activity:

• Formal evaluation of the mentee's performance. The mentor is not the supervisor of the mentee; the mentor serves as an adviser and coach, not an evaluator.

• Confidential reports to the mentee's supervisor. Mentoring requires confidentiality that allows the mentee to share what is on his or her mind without worry about repercussions. If the confidentiality of the relationship is breached, the mentee will lose trust in the mentor.

• Comments or opinions on the mentee's leadership ability. Openly discussing the mentee's ability to lead beyond the private conversations of mentee and mentor is a serious breach of the confidentiality of the relationship.

PITFALLS IN MENTORING

Areas for caution in the development of mentoring protocols are further elucidated by Crow & Matthews (1998) in their "pitfalls in mentoring." Here are the pitfalls and our explanations about each one:

- Mentors may have personal agendas. It is inappropriate for mentors to project the way they ran their schools and what served them when the context of the mentee's school may be totally different. There is no "one best way" to lead a school, nor is there one best kind of leadership. The mentee may be a very different leader than the mentor.
- Relationships may become too protective and controlling. The mentor needs to allow the mentee to make some mistakes and to learn from them.
- Problem-solving and decision-making may be restricted by the mentor. The mentee needs to learn how to solve problems and make decisions independently. The mentor should not overstep this protocol.
- The mentor needs to know when to let the mentee make decisions on his or her own and solve a problem on his or her own. It should be noted that Vermont mentors are trained to become directive only if they sense or know the school leader is going to do something that might result in a job-actionable decision, such as misusing power or using verbally abusive language (Gimbel & Kefor, 2018, p. 7). Mentor programs need to be cognizant of this.
- The mentoring relationship itself may create dependency. The mentor needs to know when to "wean" the mentee as the mentee gains skill and confidence. By the same token, if the mentee does not seem to be quick to adopt approaches suggested by the mentor, the mentor should not exhibit any behavior which would make the mentee lose self-confidence.
- Mentors might encourage cloning. It is important that the mentor allow the mentee to be him- or herself—to implement any suggestions the mentor offers in the manner that feels most comfortable and personally authentic to the mentee.

SUGGESTIONS OF FOCAL POINTS
FOR MENTOR MEETINGS

Taking into consideration the suggested actions for the mentoring process and possible pitfalls, effective mentor meetings should not become perfunctory check-ins, but rather meaningful conversations wherein both the mentor and the mentee are building mutual understanding and trust. Together, the mentor and the mentee need to feel comfortable sharing, allowing for a mutual learning opportunity. Here are some suggestions for mentors to create meaningful conversations around learning and about trust-building (SmartBrief, February 20, 2020). We have added some details to enhance the suggestions.

1. Keep the focus on goals by taking the time early in the relationship to develop long-term objectives focused on what the mentee needs to learn to develop. Develop a plan to address the areas of focus. Massachusetts mentors are encouraged to meet with their mentees over the summer to prepare them for the opening of school and all that goes with it.

2. Choose which administrator standards on which to focus and how to meet them in accordance with the superintendent's expectations and within the context of the school and the district.

3. Measure progress by learning, not just by accomplishments. Use student achievement data to guide instructional leadership and to assess progress—but mentors should encourage new principals to be present in the instructional life of the school to gather the kinds of observational, anecdotal, and even intuitive "data" that can add a critical school-culture context to decision-making.

4. Measure progress by what the mentee learns along the way. Take a step back to reflect on the successes in the mentee's leadership and why these came about. Massachusetts and Vermont mentors are encouraged to recommend and where possible to provide time for reflection on daily practice.

5. Encourage feedback. As discussed in chapter 2, the role of feedback in the development of leadership style and practice is huge. The mentor must talk with the mentee about the need to be honest with each other so both the mentor and the mentee can offer and receive constructive and useful feedback. Helping the mentee develop his or her ability to receive feedback depends on cultivating a nonjudgmental, trusting relationship where both parties feel safe to share.

6. Acknowledge to the mentee that some learning will inevitably and necessarily take place in the job itself, even with solid leadership training that the mentee may have received prior to accepting the position. Being

able to consider and reflect with a mentor during this on-the-job training validates the role of the mentor as a guide and a resource in the learning process.

In the next chapter, we will explore the public role of school principals and how mentorship can help to build further trust in public education and school leaders.

Chapter 11

The Importance of Public
Trust in Principals

Today's divided political and social climate is causing people to reduce their circles of trust, the foundation of any healthy and successful relationship (Conley, 2019). For people in positions of leadership, like school principals, trust is essential to building a culture of collegiality and shared leadership.

A 2019 survey from the Pew Research Center identified principals as the most trusted leaders in our country's most prominent institutions. A large percentage of the 10,618 survey respondents reported confidence that K–12 public school principals care about others, provide fair and accurate information to the public, and handle resources responsibly (Bartoletti, 2019). These findings reinforce the common assumption that school principals are respected in their communities and that Americans generally believe that principals have their students' best interests in mind (Jacobson, 2019). In order to maintain the public trust in principals, we need to be sure that new principals have mentors who can be present to offer advice and promote growth in the many complex areas that pertain to the trust that the public has vested in public school principals.

One major reason for sustaining and growing the public's trust in principals is the need to discourage principal turnover, which is often caused when a situation or issue so impairs a principal's credibility—in the community or even in him or herself—that they can no longer remain in the job. As we have noted, nearly one in five principals in public schools leave their positions annually, and that rate is even higher in schools in high-poverty districts, according to 2016–2017 data from the US Department of Education's National Center for Education Statistics (Schaffhauser, 2019).

National Association of Secondary School Principals and the Learning
Policy Institute research we cited early in this book (De La Rosa, 2020) notes
that nearly half of all current principals are considering leaving their positions. These principals cite, among other reasons, a lack of access to professional development and learning opportunities that could better prepare them
to face the range of challenges that come with leading a public school.

Principals decide within the very first years of their tenure whether the job
is so overwhelming that they must leave their position. With research citing
leadership stability as an essential element in the success of school improvement initiatives, new principals need to feel professionally supported as they
do their increasingly complex jobs (Gimbel & Kefor, 2018, p. 2) in order to
maintain and improve school quality nationwide. Without access to adequate
professional development programs, such as formal mentoring, focused on
building specific capacities, principals cannot begin their new careers from
positions of strength and confidence.

A trained past principal can leverage his or her own experience in developing problem-solving strategies with a new principal, offering support that
help can ease and acclimate the new principal into the leadership role. Effective mentoring also promotes reflection and self-analysis, which can build a
new principal's self-understanding and sense of efficacy. As we have seen
throughout this book, having a veteran principal observe and comment on
the new principal's practice offers an objective, outside perception. In a way,
having a mentor helps a principal with translating textbook theory into real-
world practice (Smith & Piele, 2006, p. 118).

Principal mentorship, as we have noted previously, has not often been the
subject of rigorous research, nor does the practice yet have a well-developed
theoretical foundation (p. 118). Moreover, clear trends in mentoring programs
are not apparent. It is our contention that fully developed, formal, and district-
or state-supported mentorship programs, by enhancing principal competency,
can play a significant and definable role in school improvement by reducing
school leadership turnover that can in turn help reduce teacher turnover.

By creating more stable communities of educators, mentorship programs
can have indirect but powerful effects on

- strategic and classroom-level school improvement efforts;
- the development of collaborative professional cultures within schools; and

- the building of sustained and effective relationships among all school and community constituencies, thus creating more comprehensive support for the work of the school and its teachers.

Even some "established" mentorship programs shortcut what we see as the basic elements of truly effective initiatives. Based on our research in preparing this book, we believe that it is imperative that new principals have access to trained mentors.

BOOK ECHOES: TRUST, COMMUNICATION, LISTENING, WORK–LIFE BALANCE

Being able to unburden him or herself by conversing with a mentor allows a new principal a chance to participate in a culture of shared leadership to make an impact on teaching and learning. This "unburdening" may also help diminish the stress associated with being a new principal and, in turn, help to reduce the scourge of high principal turnover.

Throughout this book there are reminders of what actions/behaviors are important for new principals to establish in their leadership practices. The judgment required to take effective actions that lead to personal and school success is usually acquired in practice. Without time for principals to reflect on how to incorporate these behaviors into practice, the new principal may not realize the impact of his/her behavior. The luxury of having an experienced, trained mentor as a mirror or sounding board can provide the new principal opportunities to contemplate how to build trust, to communicate effectively, and to listen actively in order to learn what is on the minds of teachers, students, parents, and the community.

Our next chapter focuses on the National Association of Secondary School Principals (NASSP) Association's June 2020 policy recommendations to better support and prepare principals for the complex job of school leadership. The association offers recommendations for federal and state policymakers as well as for district leaders and school leaders themselves.

Chapter 12

About the NASSP and Learning Policy Institute Research

The National Association of Secondary School Principals (NASSP) and the Learning Policy Institute partnered in 2019–2020 to conduct research on causes and impact of principal turnover in the United States. They released a report based upon their multiphase project in May of 2020.

The report examines reasons why principals leave their positions, and the findings help inform policy recommendations at the federal, state, and local levels. This multiphase research project was conducted to identify the causes and consequences of principal turnover. The purpose of the project was to increase awareness of this issue and to identify and share evidence-based responses to help mitigate excessive turnover in the principal profession. The project was conducted in three phases (National Association of Secondary School Principals [NASSP], May 14, 2020).

KEY FINDINGS AND HOW THEY RELATE TO THIS BOOK

Among the key findings of this project are those that relate to topics included in this book. The two most closely connected are work–life balance and inadequate access to professional learning opportunities.

1. *Working conditions* relate to work–life balance. Those principal respondents who claimed that they were going to leave their schools blamed

their heavy workload. The burden of not having adequate support for students as well as for themselves leaves principals stressed.

2. *Inadequate access to professional learning opportunities* connects with mentoring. Focus group and survey responses suggest that many principals face obstacles in finding and accessing professional learning opportunities. A large percentage of principals cited lack of time and funding for professional development. These responses resonate with some of the reasons why mentoring of new principals is not widespread.

IMPLICATIONS FOR POLICY AND PRACTICE LOCAL LEVEL

One of the implications for policy and practice locally is the demonstrated need to "create or sustain helpful mechanisms for principal feedback, evaluation and mentoring. Districts that support, develop, and mentor principals can reduce the likelihood of principal attrition. District leaders can examine the usefulness of their principal support and evaluation systems, gathering input from principals as well as others in the district and community with an eye toward sustaining practices that are helpful and creating new mechanisms and supports as needed" (NASSP, May 14, 2020).

Another implication that pertains to our thesis in this book is a recommendation that states "remove barriers to principal professional development. As districts review principal workload, they should consider time for professional development. District leaders can consider providing district staff support to free up principals' time, offering professional development at times and locations convenient for principals, and working professional learning into the district feedback, evaluation, and mentoring system. Districts and schools can use both local funds and federal funds under Every Student Succeeds Act (ESSA), Title II, Part A . . .." (NASSP, May 14, 2020).

A third implication pertains to principals' working conditions and school needs. District leaders should be alert to principals' workloads and seek to ensure that school administrative teams are properly staffed and that support personnel are in place for effectively addressing students' social and emotional needs (NASSP, May 14, 2020).

IMPLICATIONS FOR POLICY AND PRACTICE
STATE AND FEDERAL LEVEL

According to the NASSP 2020 report, many states gather data about teacher working conditions via surveys, school improvement plans, and district and school report cards. NASSP suggests gathering this information for all principals and aggregating it at the state level to inform policy decisions.

By increasing state and federal investments in high-quality professional development, more states are beginning to make commitments to funding principal professional learning opportunities through coaching, mentoring, and networks. Many states are also taking the opportunity to allocate funding from Title II, Part A of ESSA to evidence-based professional development. Nearly half of states are taking advantage of the optional 3 percent set aside to invest in principal learning. At this writing, ESSA is supposed to be reauthorized in 2020, and its funding could be used to further support school principals and mentoring programs (NASSP, 2020).

TOP BENEFITS OF MENTORING

It seems that mentoring is becoming more important in helping reduce principal turnover. If funds are set aside for mentoring programs and if adequate support is available for principals to have time to devote to mentoring, then perhaps the 42 percent rate of principals who are considering leaving their positions will decrease (De La Rosa, 2020). A school leader's departure impacts teaching and learning. The cost of replacement involves time and money.

In addition to potentially curbing principal attrition, investing in formal mentorship offers other benefits. The greatest of these is simply having someone available to whom a new principal can ask questions and from whom they receive advice. While all this advice may not be taken, the mentor can help the principal sort out which matters are of utmost importance. One new principal said, "Had I known what my weaknesses were beforehand, I could have worked on them." A mentor can offer a new window into a problem or situation from a perspective the new principal may not have considered.

Mentors can help principals improve communication skills by observing how the teachers and staff understand the directions the new principal offers.

Another new principal said the best advice she received was that "it's all about how you treat people. I can bring you in and give you a reprimand, but it's how I give you the reprimand" that matters (Superville, 2019).

The freedom to vent with someone the new principal trusts is one of the biggest benefits of having a mentor. By talking things out with the mentee, the mentor can help the new principal identify and address sources of frustration (Morley, 2019). Moreover, since the mentor is a retired principal and has experience, the mentor can suggest some strategies the new principal may not have thought about. Knowing that he or she has aired a matter with a credible, trustworthy mentor can give the new principal confidence going into difficult situations. This confidence may lead to better decisions (Morley, 2019).

Finally, the one-on-one mentoring relationship can boost morale for both the mentor and the new principal. By helping others, mentors can improve their own skills and may be inspired by new ideas and learn new strategies from their mentees (Morley, 2019).

Having had a trained mentor who has taken an interest in their leadership skills and growth helps new principals become more reflective in their practice. This reflection helps them to identify skill areas for growth and plan a pathway to improve their leadership skills.

EFFECTIVE MENTOR CHARACTERISTICS REDUX

To again sum up what we know about effective mentoring, states and districts looking to establish a corps of principal mentors should seek mentor candidates with these qualities:

- A willingness to invest time and energy in the professional development of their colleagues
- A strong conviction and belief that other administrators are likely to have a positive effect on the quality of schooling
- Confidence in their own abilities to mentor/coach as well as lead
- Possession of high standards and expectations for their own abilities and for the work of their colleagues
- A belief that mentoring is a mutually enhancing professional development opportunity in which both partners will achieve satisfaction from the relationship (Maine Principals' Association, 2015–2016).

THE JOYS OF BEING A MENTOR

Recently retired principals make a logical and ideal candidate pool of principal mentors, and the reflections of those who have become part of mentor corps in their own jurisdictions make a compelling case for recruiting from this pool. Experience, wisdom, generosity of spirit, and a desire to continue to offer service are strong motivators, and we leave you here with these reports from experienced principal mentors in the State of Maine:

- "As a retiree, having a mentee allows me to use my expertise and give back to another person just starting out."
- "I cannot overstate the learning I have had around being a stronger listener and understanding that supporting someone means listening and questioning and not always answering or dictating."
- "Having a mentee is an expanding experience. You get a peek into another school's culture, and it forces you to be reflective about your own work."
- "I am by nature a problem solver, and this work forces me to sit back and encourage my mentee to find solutions. In fact, I got some unsolicited feedback from a colleague recently commenting on how she appreciated the fact that I listened and didn't just jump to problem solving."
- "This two-year mentoring program is really great for both parties. I am a better leader because of my learning through this process, and I believe that my mentee is as well. Being a principal is a job that is high impact and high stress and we must support those who are willing to take on that role" (Maine Principals' Association, 2015–2016).

References

Abitabile, A. W. (2020, January 9). *Making Teachers Stick: How School Leadership Affects Teacher Retention*. National Association of Secondary School Principals. https://www.nassp.org/2020/01/01/making-teachers-stick-january-2020/

Aldrich, M. W. (2018, August 10). *How Do You Improve Schools?* ChalkBeat Tennessee. https://tn.chalkbeat.org/2018/8/10/21105495/how-do-you-improve-schools-start-by-coaching-principals-says-new-study

Anderson, L. M., & Turnbull, B. J. (2019). *Sustaining a Principal Pipeline*. Wallace Foundation. https://www.wallacefoundation.org/knowledge-center/pages/sustainability-of-principal-pipeline-initiative.aspx

Association for Supervision and Curriculum Development. (2015, December 3). *EdPulse, ASCD SmartBrief: Which Recommendations Will Encourage Great Principals to Stay in Their Jobs Longer?* Survey results published online. www.smartbrief.com/news/ascd.

Association of Washington School Principals. (2016). *New Principal Mentoring*. http://www.awsp.org/member-support/principal-support/new-principal-mentoring

Bartoletti, J. (2019). The principal's greatest asset: Public trust. *NASSP*. https://www.nassp.org/2019/09/24/the-principals-greatest-asset-public-trust/

Bell, S. (2020, February). *A Principal's Playbook for Two-Way Feedback*. Association for Supervision and Curriculum Development: Education Update. http://www.ascd.org/publications/newsletters/education_update/feb20/vol62/num02/A_Principal's_Playbook_for_Two-Way_Feedback.aspx

Berg, J. H., Connolly, C., Lee, A., & Fairley, E. (2018). A matter of trust. *Educational Leadership*, *75*(6), 56–61. http://www.ascd.org/publications/educational-leadership/mar18/vol75/num06/A-Matter-of-Trust.aspx

Bloom, G. S., Castagna, C. L., Moir, E. R., & Warren, B. (2005). *Blended Coaching: Skills and Strategies to Support Principal Development*. Thousand Oaks, CA: Corwin Press.

Branch, G. F., Hanushek, E. A., & Rivkin, S. G. (2013). School leaders matter: Measuring the impact of effective principals. *Education Week, 13*(1), 62–69.

Center for Adaptive Schools. (2006). *The Seven Norms of Collaborative Work.* http://theadaptiveschool.weebly.com/7-norms-of-collaborative-work.html

Cherkowski, S., & Walker, K. (2020, March 5). *Workplace Well-Being in K-12 Schools.* EdCan Network. https://www.edcan.ca/articles/flourish-at-work-fact-sheet/

Conley, R. (2019, September 5). *3 Ways to Widen Your Circle of Trust.* SmartBrief. https://www.smartbrief.com/original/2019/09/3-ways-widen-your-circle-trust

Crow, G. M., & Matthews, J. L. (1998). *Finding One's Way: How Mentoring Can Lead to Dynamic Leadership.* Thousand Oaks, CA: Corwin Press.

Daskal, L. (2020). *How to Coach a Struggling Employee.* Lolly Daskal. https://www.lollydaskal.com/leadership/how-to-coach-a-struggling-employee/

De La Rosa, S. (2020, May 14). *Report: Nearly Half of Principals Considering Leaving Their Schools.* Education Dive. https://www.educationdive.com/news/report-nearly-half-of-principals-considering-leaving-their-schools/577843/

Fain, L. (2020, February 20). *Leaders: How Mentoring Can Help Your Communication Skills.* SmartBrief. https://www.smartbrief.com/original/2020/02/leaders-how-mentoring-can-help-your-communication-skills

Gill, J. (2019, March). *Lean on Me.* Association for Supervision and Curriculum Development. http://www.ascd.org/publications/educational-leadership/mar19/vol76/num06/Lean-on-Me.aspx

Gimbel, P., & Kefor, K. (2018). Perceptions of a principal mentoring initiative. *NASSP Bulletin, 102*(1), 22–37. https://doi.org/10.1177/0192636518754405

Gimbel, P., Leana, L., & Gow, P. (2016). Role Call. *Principal Leadership, 16*(6), 17–19. https://www.nassp.org/?s=role+call+message+received%3A+the+lost+art+of+communication

Gimbel, P. A. (2003). *Solutions for Promoting Principal–Teacher Trust.* Lanham, MD: Scarecrow Press.

Gimbel, P. A., & Leana, L. (with Bird, A.) (2013). *Healthy Schools: The Hidden Component to Teaching and Learning.* Lanham: Rowland and Littlefield Education.

Goldrick, L. (2016, March). *Support from the Start: A 50-State Review of Policies on New Educator Induction and Mentoring.* https://newteachercenter.org/wp-content/uploads/2016CompleteReportStatePolicies.pdf

Goode, H., & Shinkle, E. (2020, January 8). *The Principal's Secret Sauce: Finding the Ideal Work-Life Balance.* Global Teletherapy. https://globalteletherapy.com/principals-secret-sauce-finding-work-life-balance/

Heifetz, R., & Linsky, M. (2002, June). *A Survival Guide for Leaders.* Harvard Business Review. https://hbr.org/2002/06/a-survival-guide-for-leaders

Hoff, N. (2019, August 14). *How to Give Feedback Like a Boss*. SmartBrief. https://www.smartbrief.com/original/2019/08/how-give-feedback-boss

Jacobson, L. (2019, September 19). *Survey: K-12 Principals Most Trusted to be Ethical, Responsible*. Education Dive. https://www.educationdive.com/news/survey-k-12-principals-most-trusted-to-be-ethical-responsible/563105/

Jentz, B. (2009). First time in a position of authority. *Phi Delta Kappan, 91*(1), 56–60. http://www.pdkmembers.org/members_online/publications/archive/pdf/k0909jen.pdf

Johanek, M. C., & Spero, K. (2019, November 13). *The Silent Crisis of Leadership in Education*. SmartBrief. https://www.smartbrief.com/original/2019/11/silent-crisis-leadership-education#:~:text=There%20is%20a%20silent%20crisis%20undermining%20school%20improvement%20efforts.&text=However%2C%20in%20educational%20leadership%2C%20the,faced%20by%20leaders%20in%20education

Jones, J., & Vari, T. J. (2019, March). *Role Call: Cut Out the 'Culture of Nice' in Providing Feedback*. National Association of Secondary School Principals. https://www.nassp.org/2019/03/01/role-call-march-2019/

Kohm, B., & Nance, B. (2013). Creating collaborative cultures. *Educational Leadership, 67*(2), 67–72.

Leithwood, K. (2005). *Educational Leadership: A Review of the Research*. Temple University Center for Research in Human Development and Education. https://files.eric.ed.gov/fulltext/ED508502.pdf

Leithwood, K., Louis, K. C., Anderson, S., & Wahlstrom, K. (2004). *How Leadership Influences Student Learning*. New York: The Wallace Foundation. http://www.wallacefoundation.org/knowledge-center/school-leadership/key-research/Documents/How-Leadership-Influences-Student-Learning.pdf

Levin, S., & Bradley, K. (2019, March 19). *Understanding and Addressing Principal Turnover: A Review of the Research*. Learning Policy Institute. https://learningpolicyinstitute.org/product/nassp-understanding-addressing-principal-turnover-review-research-report

Levin, S., Scott, C., Yang, M., Leung, M., & Bradley, K. (2020, May 14). *Supporting a Strong, Stable Principal Workforce: What Matters and What Can Be Done*. National Association of Secondary School Principals. https://learningpolicyinstitute.org/product/supporting-strong-stable-principal-workforce-report

Maine Department of Education. (n.d.). *Induction and Mentoring*. https://www.maine.gov/doe/educators/educatoreval/inductionmentoring

Manna, P. (2015). *Developing Excellent School Principals to Advance Teaching and Learning: Considerations for State Policy*. New York: Wallace Foundation. https://www.wallacefoundation.org/knowledge-center/pages/developing-excellent-school-principals.aspx

Massachusetts Department of Elementary and Secondary Education. (2015a). *Educator Licensure and Preparation Program Approval Regulations.* https://www.doe.mass.edu/lawsregs/603cmr7.html?section=02

Massachusetts Department of Elementary and Secondary Education. (2015b). *Professional Standards for Administrative Leadership.* https://www.doe.mass.edu/lawsregs/603cmr7.html?section=10

Massachusetts Department of Elementary and Secondary Education. (2015c). *Standards for Induction Programs for Administrators.* https://www.doe.mass.edu/lawsregs/603cmr7.html?section=02

Massachusetts School Administrators Association. (2018). *Self-titled Brochure.*

Massachusetts School Administrators Association. (2019, January). *Conference.*

Massachusetts School Administrators Association. (2020). *Massachusetts Mentor Survey.* Survey results published online.

Medium. (2019, March 20). *What's Most Important in Risk Communication?* https://sharpcloud.medium.com/whats-most-important-in-risk-communication-2e91038cc82b

Morford, L. M. (2002, April 2). *Learning the Ropes or Being Hung: Organizational Socialization Influences on New Rural High School Principals.* Research Gate. https://www.researchgate.net/publication/234681865_Learning_the_Ropes_or_Being_Hung_Organizational_Socialization_Influences_on_New_Rural_High_School_Principals

Morley, M. (2019, January 11). *Top 10 Benefits of Mentoring.* Small Business–Chron. https://smallbusiness.chron.com/top-10-benefits-mentoring-25779.html

National Association of Elementary School Principals. (2003). *Making the Case for Principal Mentoring.* Education Alliance at Brown University. https://www.brown.edu/academics/education-alliance/sites/brown.edu.academics.education-alliance/files/publications/prncpalmntrg.pdf

National Association of Elementary School Principals. (2008). *National Mentor Training and Certification Program.* https://www.naesp.org/mentor

National Association of Secondary School Principals. (2020, May 14). *With Nearly Half of Principals Considering Leaving, Research Urges Attention to Working Conditions, Compensation, and Supports.* https://www.globenewswire.com/news-release/2020/05/14/2033585/0/en/WITH-NEARLY-HALF-OF-PRINCIPALS-CONSIDERING-LEAVING-RESEARCH-URGES-ATTENTION-TO-WORKING-CONDITIONS-COMPENSATION-AND-SUPPORTS.html

National Policy Board for Educational Administration. (2015). *Professional Standards.* https://www.npbea.org/wp-content/uploads/2017/06/Professional-Standards-for-Educational-Leaders_2015.pdf

New Hampshire Association of School Principals. (2014a). *Professional Standards*. https://www.education.nh.gov/sites/g/files/ehbemt326/files/inline-documents/state -board-materials-20190912.pdf

New Hampshire Association of School Principals. (2014b). *Training Manual for New Mentors: A Professional Development Approach*. Concord, NH: Author.

NYC Leadership Academy. (2019). *Giving New Principals a Strong Start: What Works in Principal Induction*. https://www.nycleadershipacademy.org/wp-content/ uploads/2019/05/principal-induction-leadership-brief.pdf

Ontario Principals' Council. (2017). *International Symposium White Paper: Principal Work-Life Balance and Well-Being*. Toronto, ON. https://www.edu.uwo.ca/faculty-prof iles/docs/other/pollock/PrincipalWellBeing-17-FINAL-with-Acknowledgement-1.pdf

Petty, A. (2020, January 29). *Want Real Leadership Growth? Focus on Strengthening as a Communicator*. SmartBrief. https://www.smartbrief.com/original/2020/01/w ant-real-leadership-growth-focus-strengthening-communicator

Quy, L. (2019, August 21). *An Essential Skill You Need to be a Successful Leader*. SmartBrief. https://www.smartbrief.com/original/2019/08/essential-skill-you-need -be-successful-leader

RAND Corporation. (2012). *Focus on K-12 education*. https://www.rand.org/pubs/ corporate_pubs/CP613-2012-08.html

Riddell, R. (2019, December 17). *Lessons in Leadership: 4 Perspectives Taking Top Administrators to the Next Level*. Education Dive. https://www.educationdive.com/ news/lessons-in-leadership-4-perspectives-taking-top-administrators-to-the-next/ 569089/

Rowland, C. (2017). *Principal Professional Development: New Opportunities for a Renewed State Focus*. Education Policy Center at American Institutes for Research. https://files.eric.ed.gov/fulltext/ED582417.pdf

Schaffhauser, D. (2019, July 31). *Report Offers Remedies for Principal Turnover*. The Journal. https://thejournal.com/articles/2019/07/31/report-offers-remedies-for- principal-turnover.aspx

School Leaders Network. (2014, November 26). *The High Cost of Principal Turn-over*. https://www.carnegie.org/news/articles/the-high-cost-of-principal-turnover/

Shelton, S. (2012). *Preparing a Pipeline of Effective Principals: A Legislative Approach*. National Conference of State Legislatures. https://www.wallacefounda tion.org/knowledge-center/documents/preparing-a-pipeline-of-effective-principals -a-legislative-approach.pdf

Shelton, S. (2013). *Evaluating School Principals: A Legislative Approach*. National Conference of State Legislatures. https://www.ncsl.org/documents/educ/SchoolPri ncipals.pdf

Smith, S. C., & Piele, P. K. (2006). *School Leadership: Handbook for Excellence in Student Learning*. Thousand Oaks, CA: Corwin Press. https://files.eric.ed.gov/full text/ED401596.pdf

Southern Regional Education Board. (2016, May). *Getting It Right: Designing Principal Preparation Programs that Meet District Needs for Improving Low-Performance Schools*. https://www.sreb.org/publication/getting-it-right

Superville, D. R. (2015). *Data May Help Slow the Turnover of Principals*. Education Week.

Superville, D. R. (2017, September 5). *Federal Educational-Leadership Initiatives in a Budget Pickle*. Education Week. https://www.edweek.org/ew/articles/2017/09/06 /educational-leadership-initiatives-in-a-budget-pickle.html

Superville, D. R. (2019). Principal turnover is a problem. New data could help districts combat it. *Education Week, 39*(18), p. 1, 10. https://www.edweek.org/ew/arti cles/2019/12/19/principal-turnover-is-a-problem-new-data.html

Toner, M. (2019, December). *Going, Going, Gone? Research Suggests Principal Pipelines May Help More Leaders to Stay*. National Association of Secondary School Principals. https://www.nassp.org/2019/12/01/going-going-gone/

Understood for All. (2017). *Bullying*. Understood. https://www.understood.org/pages /en/friends-feelings/common-challenges/bullying/

Vermont Legislature. (2012). *Vermont Educational Community Act 20*. https://legisla ture.vermont.gov/Documents/2012/Docs/ACTS/ACT020/ACT020%20As%20En acted.pdf

Wallace Foundation. (2007). *Getting Principal Mentoring Right: Perspectives from the Field*. https://www.wallacefoundation.org/knowledge-center/Documents/Gett ing-Principal-Mentoring-Right.pdf

Weingartner, C. J. (2009). *Principal Mentoring: A Safe, Simple and Support-ive Approach*. Thousand Oaks, CA: Corwin Press. http://dx.doi.org/10.4135 /9781452219349

Wellman, B., & Lipton, L. (2003). *Making Mentoring Work: An ASCD Action Tool*. Miravia.

Whitaker, T., Good, M. W., & Whitaker, K. (2019, September). *How Principals Can Support New Teachers*. Association for Supervision and Curriculum Devel-opment. http://www.ascd.org/publications/educational-leadership/sept19/vol77/n um01/How-Principals-Can-Support-New-Teachers.aspx

Index

About the Authors

Phyllis Gimbel, EdD, having spent nearly twenty years in teaching and administrative positions in both public and independent schools, has published and presented widely on a variety of topics related to leadership, mentoring, teaching, and learning. Her second book, *Healthy Schools: The Hidden Component of Teaching and Learning,* was published in 2013, and her recent publications include an article on communication in school leadership, which was published in the hundredth anniversary issue of the journal, *Principal Leadership* and a 2018 article published in the *NASSP Bulletin,* titled, "Perceptions of a Principal Mentoring Initiative."

Dr. Gimbel received a master's in Teaching Romance Languages from Teachers College, Columbia University, a master's in Education from Harvard University, and a doctoral degree in Education from the University of Massachusetts.

Dr. Gimbel is a professor of Educational Leadership at Bridgewater State University, where she received the V. James DiNardo Alumni Award for Excellence in Teaching and was awarded the first faculty fellowship in the Office of Teaching and Learning.

Peter Gow has been a teacher and administrator in independent schools for over forty years. He is the Independent Curriculum Resource Director for One Schoolhouse, a provider of online student courses and professional development programs. A prolific blogger—for *Education Week* and other outlets as well as his own *Not Your Father's School* blog—Gow has consulted, written, and presented on topics ranging from curriculum to teaching to school operations. A third-generation teacher, he is deeply interested in teacher training and professional culture and is the author of several books on schools and teaching including *An Admirable Faculty: Recruiting, Hiring, Training, and Retaining the Best Independent School Teachers* (National Association of Independent Schools, 2005), and *The Intentional Teacher: Forging a Great Career in the Independent School Classroom* (Avocus, 2009), and *What Is a School? A Philosophical and Guide for Independent School Leaders, Trustees, and Friends* (Publish Green, 2011). Above all, Gow is committed to a belief that independent school educators have been too long absent from the national conversation on education and teaching and that it is time for them to step up in the service of all students in all kinds of schools—to listen and learn with humility and sensitivity, and to share what they have learned from their own experiences and their own perspectives.

Samson Goldstein is a middle school inclusion and substantially separate special educator at Taunton Public Schools in Massachusetts. Samson graduated with a BA from the University of Massachusetts and a master's in Special Education from Bridgewater State University. Samson is a graduate research assistant and will receive an Education Specialist (formerly CAGS) certificate in Educational Leadership in 2021.